VITTORIO SERRA

KU-739-237

NEW PRACTICAL GUIDE

VENICE

★ *110 colour illustrations*
★ *detailed map of the town*
★ *useful information*

NEW EDITION

BONECHI EDIZIONI «IL TURISMO» - FIRENZE

CONTENTS

VENICE «QUEEN OF THE ADRIATIC»

First of all, why Venice? Let us go back to the time when non-Italic Indo-Europeans settled in the Venetian plains. They very probably came from Illyria in the second millenium B.C. and over-ran the Euganean hills, founded Vicenza, Treviso, Padua, Este, Belluno and other centres. In the first century B.C., these towns were Romanized and it was at this point that the local population was given the name of Venetians. The word Venetians, if truly of Indo-European origin, could mean «noblemen»; if, on the other hand it is pre-Indo-European, its meaning would be «foreigners» or «newcomers». It is to be presumed, therefore that «newcomers» or «novi venti» led to Veneti (Venetians) and thence to Venezia (Venice).

Venice took many centuries to develop. The nucleus of the original settlement was in the area of today's Rialto district. A network of canals was planned and the earth the builders dug up, was used to strengthen the islands of the lagoon. The Grand Canal and the innumerable «rii» (lesser canals) of Venice, which by means of 400 bridges, link over 118 islets to each other today came into being over the centuries: tree-trunks were tightly bound together and used to consolidate the muddy little islands, constituting the foundations of the houses and palaces. From East to West, the town measures 4,260 metres and from North to South it is 2,790 metres wide. It covers an area of 7,062 Kmsq. and its perimeter (including the islands of the «Stazione Marittima» (The Ferry Terminal), the island of St. George, of St. Helen and the island of Giudecca is 13,700 metres.

When Venice first appears, it looks like a dream – city, springing like a gleaming splendid vision from the waters of the lagoon. Its delicate beauty changes with the seasons and unfolds countless treasures: historical places, natural beauties, art, the traditional hospitality and kindness of the people all make it a truly unique place. The famous Grand Canal or «Canalazzo», as it is called by the Venetians, with its marvellous succession of beautiful «palazzi» and picturesque houses is the main throughfare. Its inverted S winds for 3,800 metres through the town and at some points it is 30 and at others 70 metres wide; it is from 5 to 5 and a half metres deep. It flows from North-West to South-East (dividing Venice in two) into the much wider St. Mark's Canal, which reflects the sparkling bulk of the Ducal Palace. The Grand Canal, crossed by three bridges (the Railway bridge, the Rialto and the Academy bridges), together with the 45 «rii» (little canals) that flow into it, link all the «sestieri» (districts) of the town to each other.

The typical «rii» or «rielli» are mostly about 4 or 5 metres wide and can only be used by gondolas. The «rii» are nearly always flanked by narrow, twisty pathways or alleys called «calli». The calli lead into little clearings or squares called «campi» – if fairly large, or «campielli» – if small. The «rii» can also lead into little dead-ends or courtyards, called «corti».

Venice is divided into six «sestieri»: St. Mark, Castello, Cannaregio, Santa Croce, St. Paul, and Dorsoduro (which includes the parish of St. Eufemia on the island of the Giudecca). There are about 100.000 people living in the «sestieri».

Venice is 4 kms away from the mainland and is linked to it by ferry-boats, a double railway bridge (3,601 metres long and built 1841-46 and by a road bridge, built in 1931-32, which is 4,070 metres long and 20 metres wide. The two bridges run together for quite a long way.

High water in Piazzetta San Marco and the discomfort of the Venetians.

THE CLIMATE

Venice is fortunate in having a very temperate climate. As a matter of fact, the average yearly temperature is 14,4° centigrade; winter is rarely very cold and summer is not too hot; there is abundant rainfall from summer to autumn. The «grecale» hits the town in May, when this wind comes sweeping in from the Adriatic. The North-Easterly wind which hits the town in winter is sometimes called the «Bora». During the so-called high tide or «acqua alta» (high water), as the Venetians call it, the town

Gondolas sliding over Piazza San Marco thanks to "high water".

takes on a very strange appearance. As a rule, the waters invade the Piazza San Marco, rising to about half a metre above the level of the square, so that the gondolas can come rowing right into the middle of it. The poor residents have to use improvised raised platforms and gangways to get around the flooded area. These periodic floods are one of the main causes of erosion in the foundations of the various public and private buildings of Venice.

A fluttering cloud of pigeons in Piazza San Marco.

PATRON SAINT, PIGEONS AND GONDOLAS

Venice has had two Patron Saints: St. Todaro (Theodore), of Greek origin, who embodied the feeling of allegiance tributed by the newly founded Republic to the Bizantine Empire, and St. Mark the Evangelist, whose body was brought to Venice in 828 by two Venetian merchants, who had removed it from the church dedicated to him in Alexandria in Egypt (where the saint had been martyred in the times of the Roman Emperor Nero) to save it from being desecrated by the Muslims. The holy relics were received with reverence and due honour was paid to them. The Saint was proclaimed Patron and protector of the town and as his symbol is a winged lion, the Lion of St. Mark became the town's emblem.

Venice is also called «Serenissima» (most serene) because of the serene idea of justice which was the basis of all the social and political measures taken by the Government. The higher magistrates never belonged to any of the town's factions or political parties and were thus in a position to pass judgement on matters of public interest in a climate of aloof serenity. The Republic of Venice is thus nearly always represented allegorically

A gondola on the Grand Canal.

holding the two symbols of Justice: the sword and the scales.

As soon as one arrives in Piazza San Marco, one is welcomed by festive clouds of pigeons. According to an old legend, the birds were first brought to Venice from Cyprus and presented to the wife of the Doge. For the Venetians the pigeons are the traditional ornament of the lovely square and are cared for by the Town Hall authorities, who see that they get a plentiful ration of corn every morning at nine plus another allowance at one P.M. During the tourist season, the pigeons receive supplementary rations from the innumerable visitors who hold out corn to feed them in order to be photographed amidst a whirling cloud of fluttering wings. But tourists are also fascinated by the gondolas that slide elegantly and silently along the waters of the Grand Canal or along one of the twisty «rii», evoking all kinds of romantic daydreams. As we are on the subject of gondolas, let us see where the word comes from. According to Mutinelli's «Lessico Veneto» (Venetian Lexicon), «gondola» comes from «cymbula» – a small boat. The gondola is a small, asymmetrical, flat-bottomed rowing boat, generally possessing a single skull which is rowed from a standing position. The overall length is about four or five metres and the width about one metre fifty. The first gondolas appeard towards the end of the XIIIth Cent., but we do not know who invented them.

Above: view of the auditorium from the stage of La Fenice, one of the greatest Italian temples of "bel canto". Opera productions of La Fenice are of international interest; below: one of the many craft that takes part in the Historical Boat Race (Regata Storica) streams along the Grand Canal on the Ist Sunday of September, amidst crowds of onlookers.

Above and below: the famous Carnival of Venice which has inspired so many composers and artists: thousands of visitors flock to Venice every year to take part in the festivities, involving the whole town.

ARCHITECTURAL STYLES

There are four main architectural styles in Venice, which came into being during the four most glorious periods of its history: the Byzantine, the Romanesque, the Gothic and the Renaissance styles.

THE BYZANTINE STYLE – Grand, imposing, richly ornamented volume and mass flow and swell into variously shaped arches and domes. The Byzantine dome is either supported by four or eight pillars; four, when the base is square, eight when it is octagonal. Pillars are joined to each other by arches. Galleries of columns supporting the domes are essential elements in Byzantine churches. The capitals of the columns supporting the domes are essential elements in Byzantine churches. The capitals of the columns are decorated with acanthus leaves and animals and generally surmounted by richly carved «cushions» or «pulvini». The walls, both inside and out, as well as the vaults are richly and splendidly covered with mosaics. This style flourished in Venice from the VIth to the XIIth Cents.

THE ROMANESQUE STYLE – The style prevalently adopted all over the West at the beginning of the Middle Ages by the Roman Catholic nations. In Venice, its presence is subordinate to the Byzantine style of the XIth and XIIth Cents. It is easily recognizable, because of the thickness of the walls and the diminutive size of the windows. Inside, double lines of columns or pillars, joined to each other by rounded arches, divide the churches longitudinally into three sections. The cross-vaulting is reminiscent of the Byzantine style.

THE GOTHIC STYLE – Originally the word «Gothic» meant «barbarous». The Renaissance artists in Italy called the style that flourished in Italy and in Venice between the XIIth and XVth Cents. «Gothic» because it no longer conformed to the severe rules of Classical architecture. The definition was later adopted by other nations. The style originated in the North of France in the XIIth Cent. It is distinguished by ogival arches, soaring verticality, daring, airy vaulting, flying buttresses, tall, mullioned windows divided by little columns and decorated with chiselled fretwork and geometrical ornamentation.

THE RENAISSANCE STYLE – During the first half of the XVth Cent., architects reverted to the pure, severe Greek and Roman lines, adapting them to the requirements of their times. Most important Renaissance aspects are the ground plans of the churches which recall the lines of Roman basilicas and the vaults and domes (supported by cylindrical drums) topped by lanterns with small windows; the columns are generally ungrouped and the arches rounded, cornices and trabeations are decorated with carved or painted friezes. Richly ornamented (painted or carved) coffered ceilings, splendidly framed rectangular windows, often flanked by pilasters or columns. The richness of the decorations sometimes (specially towards the late-Renaissance period) assumes exaggerated proportions, producing the so-called **Baroque** style, in which curved prevail over straight lines and unusual, bizarre decoration affects every architectural element, untramelled by preconceived formulae.

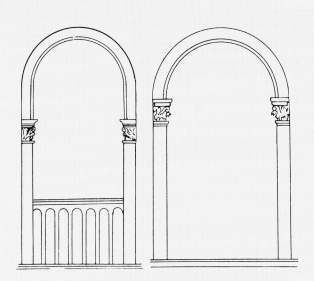

Byzantine style.   Romanesque style.

Gothic style.   Renaissance style.

THE GRAND CANAL

Left: **the Historical Boat Race near the Rialto bridge;** above: **the waterbus (vaporetto) landing at the railway station of Santa Lucia.**

ARRIVAL IN VENICE

Everyone who drives to Venice has to park in the **Piazzale Roma**, which is the huge parking lot and bus terminal for the buses linking the city to the mainland towns. The Piazzale is connected to the mainland by the **Ponte della Libertà** erected in 1933 alongside the 1876 railway bridge.
The building of the bridge and Piazzale was made necessary by the impelling need to facilitate both cargo and tourist connections with the mainland. Turning our backs on Piazzale Roma, we are now ready to enter the heart of the city by way of its main «thoroughfare», the Grand Canal. The most widely-used means of getting around in Venice is the *vaporetto* (water bus). Vaporetto service along the Grand Canal dates back to 1881. Proceeding along the **Rio Nuovo** and the **Papadopoli Gardens** we reach the **Pontile di Santa Chiara** (embarking station) on the **Fondamenta Santa Chiara** where we take a vaporetto for a scenic ride along the Grand Canal.

THE GRAND CANAL

The Church of San Simeone Piccolo; the Scalzi bridge in the distance.

The Grand Canal, shaped like a huge upside down «S» bisecting the city, is almost 2¼ miles long, 15 feet deep, and ranges from about 100 to 225 feet across.

Its aqueous «paving» sparkles in the sunlight, although the water is sometimes wave-capped and can even become sombre and menacing, depending on the weather and the season. Lining the canal on either side is a parade of incredible buildings, brightly colored little houses alongside imposing stone palaces, dating from every period and exemplifying every architectural style.

Even the most distracted sightseer cannot help but be enthralled by the vision of charming buildings, squares, tiny canals extending into the shadows, gardens stolen from the threatening grasp of the sea, and a lovely gateway here and there, blackened and corroded by the weather and the water. It is no wonder that painters and poets, musicians and writers have always expressed such great admiration for the canal. Byron, Canova, Wagner, Hemingway, among hundreds of others, all spent lengthy periods of their lives on or near its banks.

Immediately to our left we note the **Santa Lucia Station**. The railway station was named after the Palladian church dedicated to St. Lucy originally on the site, which was torn down in the middle of the 19th century to make way for the railroad linking Venice to the mainland. The railway bridge, officially inaugurated in 1846, was quite an engineering feat itself: 225 spans are supported by 75,000 pylons anchored in the depths of the lagoon. On the other hand, the station is actually a recent construction opened to the public in 1954. From the station, proceeding in the direction of St. Mark's, we immediately note the attractive **church of San Simeone Piccolo** (also called San Simeone e Giuda) just to right of the station building.

The most striking part of the church is its huge copper dome and lantern, surmounted by a statue of Christ the Redeemer, whose distinctive green colour is due to the effects of weathering. The church dominates the whole first stretch of the Grand Canal, with its impressive staircase leading down to the water. Framing the entrance is an 18th century neo-Classical porch with Corinthian columns, designed by Giovanni Scalfarotto. The majestic gable crowning it is adorned with scenes of the martyrdom of saints Simeon and Judas sculpted by Francesco Penso. The first bridge we encounter on our way to St. Mark's is the **Ponte degli Scalzi**, also known as the Station Bridge. Made entirely of white Istrian stone, it was designed by Eugenio Miozzi and put up in 1934 to replace a metal structure built in 1858 by the Lombard-Venetian city administration. The single span bridge is approximately 130 feet long and rises approximately 23 feet above water level. On the left bank by the bridge we note the imposing Baroque façade of the **church of Santa Maria di Nazareth** (or Santa Maria degli Scalzi). Keeping our eyes riveted to the left side, our glance encounters the apse and belfry of the **church of San Geremia** which was first built in the 13th century and later remodeled in 1760. Its Romanesque belltower dates back to the 13th century and is thus one of the oldest in the city. Alongside the church is a grandiose 18th century patrician palace, the **Palazzo Labia** whose interior was frescoed by Tiepolo. On the far corner is a statue of *St. John Nepomucenus* commissioned by one of the ladies of the Labia family. Still keeping our eyes to the left, just beyond the statue of the saint we see the beginning of the **Cannaregio Canal**, the second largest in Venice after the Grand Canal. Farther on, this time on the right, is one of the most celebrated buildings in the Venetian Byzantine style, the **Fondaco dei Turchi**. The building was totally (and very arbitrarily) remodelled in the 19th century on the site of the 12th-13th century palace which was once the headquarters and trade center of the Oriental merchants stationed in Venice. Today it is the **Museum of Natural History**.

Once we have passed the **Rio della Maddalena** we encounter on the left **Palazzo Vendramin Calergi**, an outstanding example of Renaissance architecture. Begun by Coducci and completed by Lombardo in 1509, it was where Richard Wagner died on February 13, 1883. A series of fine palaces follows. The first is the 17th century **Palazzo Rouda**, with its completely remodelled façade. Just beyond we note the 16th century **Palazzo Gussoni-Grimani della Vida** attributed to Sanmicheli. Originally a fresco by Tintoretto adorned its façade, but like all other outdoor murals in Venice, this one too, corroded by brine and weathering, has been lost to us. Next we see the **Palazzetto De Lezze** with its tiny façade overgrown with vines, the 17th century **Palazzo Boldù** with its rusticated stone ground-floor, and lastly the **Palazzo Contarini-Pisani**, 17th century as well, with its spacious portico on the canal side. Opposite these buildings is the majestic **Ca' Pesaro** acclaimed as Baldassarre Longhena's masterpiece of privately-commissioned architecture, and built between 1679 and 1710. So great did

Fondaco dei Turchi.

the building costs seem at the time that the architect is said to have died from worrying about whether the project would ever be finished. The imposing façade rises upon a rusticated stone base surmounted by a double tier of windows set off by clusters of columns. The building today houses the International Gallery of Modern Art and the Oriental Art Museum. On the same side, right by the Ca' Pesaro, is the **Palazzo Corner della Regina**, a Classical style building designed by Domenico Rossi (1724) on the site of the pre-existing Palazzo Cornaro. Today it is the headquarters of a bank-connected organization. Continuing along the left, we soon reach the most celebrated of the many remarkable buildings lining the Grand Canal, the **Ca' d'Oro**. After having been remodelled time and time again (and not always wisely) and passed from owner to owner, it came into the possesion of Baron Giorgio Franchetti who in 1916 donated the palace along with the art collection bearing his name to the Italian state. The façade, which today is white, was originally gilded and this gave it its name–Ca' d'Oro, in fact, means Golden House. Built around 1440 for a nobleman, Marino Contarini, in a style which combines Byzantine influence with the Gothic pointed arch motifs, it looks like charming lace embroidery rising out of the Grand Canal.

On the ground floor is a portico which, except for the central round arch, is composed of graceful pointed arches. The two upper floors have

Ca' Pesaro.

delicately pierced loggias. The righthand section of the façade is more compact with fewer empty spaces, but it is in no way less elegant than the left side. Surmounting the façade is a crown of finely-wrought crenellation. On the left is another palace, the **Palazzo Sagredo**, a late 14th century Gothic building, with an elaborate façade. Across the canal, we cannot help but notice a two storey brick structure jutting out a bit from the other buildings. This is the **Pescheria**, or **Fish Market**, which was built in 1907 by Domenico Rupolo after a design by the painter Cesare Laurenti. It opens on the Grand Canal by means of a spacious portico of slightly-pointed arches resting on columns which support a slanting roof to form the huge open loggia.

The building rises on the site of what has always been Venice's fish market. On the opposite side of the canal once more, we can make out the **Palazzo Michiel dalle Colonne**, with its distinctive ground floor colon-nade. The denomination «of the Columns», is thought by some to derive from these very columns, whereas others believe it was added to the Michiel name because it was a member of the family who actually brought the columns standing on the Piazzetta of St. Mark's from the Orient. Immediately after the Pescheria, again on the right bank, we see the impressive façade of the **Fabbriche Nuove di Rialto**.

The building was put up in 1552 by Jacopo Sansovino and occupied by

public offices having to do with trade and commerce. A bit beyond the Fabbriche Nuove we are struck by the colorful bustle of the open-air fruit and vegetable market. The building bordering the marketplace, known as the **Fabbriche Vecchie di Rialto** was erected by Scarpagnino in 1522 as the seat of the court house.

Facing the two *Fabbriche* is the Ca' Da Mosto. One of the most picturesque in Venice, this Venetian Byzantine-style palace was built in the 13th century. The Grand Canal now curves right and we are left speechless by the sight which meets our eyes upon passing the curve: before us is the Ponte di Rialto, or Rialto Bridge, in all its splendor. (We shall soon discuss it in greater detail). Beforehand, let us stop an instant and take a look at the **Fondaco dei Tedeschi** (German Storehouse) to our left.

The building we see today was built in 1515 over the site of a pre-existing structure destroyed in a fire. It was designed by Scarpagnino in the Renaissance style with a spacious round-arch portico on the ground floor and a border of white crenellation on top.

Unfortunately, nothing remains of the frescoes by Giorgione and Titian that originally adorned the façade. To the right is the **Palazzo dei Camerlenghi**, which was originally the Treasury of the Republic of St. Mark's and thus the city's financial center. The building was erected in the early 16th century by Guglielmo Bergamasco. And thus we have reached the bridge which is one of the most famous, if not the most famous, in the whole world, the **Rialto Bridge**.

Above: **the Fish Market (Pescheria)**; below: **Fabbriche Nuove di Rialto**; left: **Ca' d'Oro.**

19

Above: **Fabbriche Vecchie di Rialto**; below: **Fondaco dei Te-deschi**.

The Rialto bridge.

THE RIALTO BRIDGE

This is one of the best places to view the Grand Canal from in all its charm. The Rialto is the oldest of the three bridges spanning the canal. Originally made of wood, it caved in in 1440 and was rebuilt, again of wood, but this time with the addition of several shops along it. It had a special mechanism which allowed the middle section to be raised, whereby even the tallest masted ships could sail through. It was somewhat unstable, though, and thus in the 16th century it was decided to build a new bridge. A competition was called, attracting the participation of such well-known architects as Michelangelo, Palladio, and Sansovino, all of whom worked on the project for years. Antonio Da Ponte, a relatively unknown architect in such illustrious company, was awarded the contract and designed the bridge which was not finished until 1592. The Rialto is a single span bridge whose span measures 90 feet (the narrowest crossing of the Grand Canal is here) and has a maximum height of 24 feet at the middle. The two ends rest upon 12,000 pylons sunk into the muddy depths. The twenty-four shops lining the bridge are separated by a double arcade from which you can walk out onto the terraces.

Ca' Foscari.

Just beyond the Rialto Bridge, on the right, is the **Palazzo dei Dieci Savi**, an early 16th century Renaissance building designed by Scarpagnino. Farther ahead on the left bank are the 13th century **Palazzo Loredan** and the 12th century **Palazzo Farsetti** (today the Venice Town Hall), typical examples of the Venetian Byzantine style. The lower floors, are characterized by graceful elongated arches running the length of the ground and second floors. The upper floors and balconies date from a 16th century alteration. On the same side, just a bit ahead, is a remarkable 16th century Renaissance building, Sanmicheli's masterpiece, the **Palazzo Grimani**. Today, the three-storey palace with its handsome arcading, is occupied by the Venice Court of Appeals. On the right bank is the **Palazzo Papadopoli**, a 16th century building designed by Giacomo dei Grigi in the Classical style. Next comes a fine 15th century Gothic palace, **Palazzo Bernardo**, in which the Duke of Milan, Francesco Sforza, resided for some time. Past the Rio San Polo on the right bank, is an impressive 15th century building, the **Palazzo Pisani** with an intricate decorative motif adorning the center windows. Proceeding on the right, is the **Palazzo Balbi**, also known as «*Palazzo in volta de Canal*» (Palace on the Canal bend). Here the Grand Canal swings leftward and, on the right, by the Rio Ca' Foscari, is a famous 15th century Gothic building, the **Ca' Foscari**. Commissioned by Doge Francesco Foscari who ruled the Republic for over thirty years, it is now the Economics and Business School of the University of Venice.

The façade of Ca' Foscari has been acclaimed as one of the finest and best-proportioned in all of Venice. On the ground floor, six plain arched windows flank the great portal, while the upper floors are adorned with beautiful carved loggias whose lacy designs become more intricate with

Palazzo Grassi.

each storey. A bit farther along the left bank rises the 18th century **Palazzo Grassi**, built in 1718 by Giorgio Massari for the Grassi family of Bologna, and now occupied by the **Costume Institute**. The Classical façade has a rusticated stone ground floor and plain windows set off by simple balconies running the length of the two upper floors. Opposite Palazzo Grassi on the right bank is a beautiful example of Venetian Classical architecture, the **Palazzo Rezzonico**. The ground and second floors were designed by Baldassarre Longhena who actually started construction in 1660 commissioned by the Priuli-Bon family. The building then came into the ownership of the Rezzonico family, who commissioned Giorgio Massari, the same architect we just met working on Palazzo Grassi, to finish it, although it was not fully completed until 1747. The façade has a rusticated stone ground floor, while the two upper stories are adorned with balconies and columns which set off the individual windows. Inside the palace is the Museum of 18th century Venice. A bit farther on to the right is the 15th century Gothic **Palazzo Loredan dell'Ambasciatore** with its handsome façade. Inside the niches on either side are the 15th century Lombard sculptures. Facing Palazzo Loredan is another 15th century Gothic building, **Palazzo Falier**, characterized by loggias on either side. We have now reached the last of the three bridges spanning the Grand Canal, the **Ponte dell'Accademia**.

This bridge too has only a single span. It is made of wood and metal and has recently been completely restored. Before 1930, a 19th century all metal bridge, stood in its place, but it was torn down because it clashed too much with the rest of the Grand Canal's harmonious style. Beyond the bridge on the left is a turn-of-the- 19th century building, the **Palazzo Cavalli**

Ca' Rezzonico.

Franchetti whose façade was inspired by the Venetian Gothic style. On the opposite bank is another fine Gothic building, the **Palazzo Da Mula** which dates from the end of the 15th century. Farther on, on the same side, is a palace set in a lovely green park, the **Palazzo Venier dei Leoni** which houses the fabulous Guggenheim collection.

Facing it is the attractive **Casina delle Rose** (Rose House) in which two celebrated Italians, Canova, the 18th century sculptore, and D'Annunzio, the early 20th century writer, lived at various times. On the left is the headquarters of the local prefecture, **Palazzo Corner**, also known as **Ca' Granda** (Big House) whose impressive size undoubtedly gave it its nickname. Jacopo Corner commissioned the architect Sansovino to build it in 1535. Three centuries later, during the period Lombardy-Venice, it was occupied by the Austrian governor. Opposite the Ca' Granda is the **Palazzo Dario**, a Renaissance building erected by Pietro Lombardo in 1487, whose façade is adorned with multicolor decorative motifs and marble ornamentation.

Next along the left is the 15th century Venetian Gothic **Palazzo Contarini Fasan**, which has been dubbed «Desdemona's House». On the right we are struck by the sight of the majestic **church of Santa Maria della Salute** looming before us. This magnificent building is the masterpiece of Baldassarre Longhena, whose contribution to the appearance of the Grand Canal was considerable. Beyond the church is the **Punta della Dogana** upon which stands a 17th century tower surmounted by a globe supposed to bring good luck. From the 15th century onwards, duty on goods arriving from overseas was exacted on this spot.

Above: **the Accademia bridge**; below: **Ca' Granda.**

Church of Santa Maria della Salute.

We are now at the place where the Grand Canal flows into the huge stretch of water in front of St. Mark's. As soon as we get off our vaporetto at the **Pontile di San Marco**, we are standing before a Lombard-style building erected in the 15th century. In the past it was occupied first by the *Magistrato della Farina* (Flour Magistrate) then by the Academy of Painters and Sculptors (from 1756 to 1807, when it was headed by G. B. Tiepolo), and at present it is the headquarters of the Venice Port Authority. Inside is a hall with a ceiling fresco by Jacopo Guarana (1773) depicting the *Triumph of Art*. Proceeding, we soon arrive at the **Giardinetto del Palazzo Reale**. The park is on the site of the building which served as a storehouse for wheat. At the end of the garden we see the imposing **Palazzo della Zecca** designed by Sansovino in 1535. The rusticated stone arcading, Doric on the first and Ionic on the second floor, conveys an effect of stateliness and power, quite fitting for the Mint of the Republic of St. Mark's. Here, in fact the Venetians minted their celebrated *Zecchini d'oro* (gold sequins), the counterpart of the equally-renowned gold florins of Florence, both of which were widely circulated throughout Europe and even in the Orient.

HISTORIC CENTRE

Piazzetta di San Marco.

PIAZZETTA DI SAN MARCO

The Piazzetta serves as the simple but elegant antechamber to the grandiose Piazza San Marco. Two of the city's foremost monuments face onto it: the Doges' Palace to the east and the Libreria Sansoviana to the west. Originally, a market for foodstuffs occupied this area, but then in 1536 the reigning doge decreed that the space should be kept clear.

By the quay are two monolithic columns (one with the Lion of St. Mark's and the other with a statue of St. Theodore), both brought to Venice from the Orient in 1125. The two columns were set up on this spot in 1172 by a certain Niccolò Starantonio who had previously built one of the earliest wooden Rialto Bridges. The statue of St. Theodore (Todaro, in dialect) the first patron saint of Venice, standing atop the column, is actually a collage of different parts from different palaces, whereas the bronze lion on the second column is believed to be of Eastern, some even claim Chinese, origin. The Piazzetta was also the scene of public executions and between these columns both humble citizens and high-ranking personages were dealt the death sentence. Two of them passed into history. One was Pietro Faziol, known as «*Il Fornaretto*» (the baker's boy) who was executed after being unjustly charged with having killed a nobleman. Since then two oil lamps have been kept burning in his memory on the façade of St. Mark's nearest the Piazzetta. The other was the Count of Carmagnola, charged with high treason and executed on the same spot.

The Library of St. Mark's (Libreria Sansoviniana).

SANSOVINO LIBRARY
(Libreria di San Marco)

The Library takes up the whole west side of the Piazzetta. Considered Sansovino's masterpiece, it was defined as «the most sumptuous ever built» by the architect Palladio, while the writer Pietro Aretino remarked that it «was beyond envy». The construction of a library to house the fabulous collection of rare books donated to the city by Cardinal Bessarione (who had been granted asylum here) was decided by the Senate of the Republic in 1536.

PIAZZA SAN MARCO

Piazza San Marco.

Piazza San Marco is the Venetians' staggeringly beautiful open-air world-famous drawing room. Throughout its long, long history it has been witness to an endless stream of human events involving people from every walk of life, from the humblest artisans to the highest-ranking authorities, all of whom had a hand in creating the precious, incomparable treasure that is Venice. Harking back to the square's origins, we shall leave the description to a long-ago chronicler, Giuseppe Tassini, whose knowledge of his native town was truly incredible. In his book entitled *Curiosità Veneziane* (Venetian Curiosities), he recounts, «in olden times the Piazza San Marco was truly rustic. It was dubbed «morso» (tough) perhaps because its terrain was harder and tougher than the surrounding area and «*brolo*» (garden) because it was grassy and bordered by trees. On the opposite banks of the Batario Canal which crossed it were the two little churches of San Teodoro and San Gemignano erected, as is well-known, by Narsetes who vanquished the Goths with the aid of the Venetian navy. At the time the Basilica of St. Mark and the Doges' Palace were going up and then, during the reign of Doge

The Clocktower seen from above.

Sebastiano Ziani (1172-1178), the Batario was filled-in and the field in front of the building flattened out so the huge space could be paved to practically where it extends today.
On either side, elegant houses with arcades running their entire length were erected. A number of them were taken over by the *procuratori di San Marco* (magistrates) from whom their present name *Procuratie* derives. In 1264 the square was repaved in bricks forming a herringbone pattern which was left untouched until 1723 when a more modern design of grey trachyte from the Euganean hills and white marble, created by Andrea Tirali, was laid out in its place. Today the square is a trapezoid measuring 569 feet in length, 266 feet on the church side, and 185 feet on the opposite side.

The Clocktower: detail of the two "Moors".

THE CLOCKTOWER

Facing the church, the Clocktower is on your left. It was built by Mauro Coducci between 1496 and 1499. The wings were added on during 1500-1506, supposedly after a design by Pietro Lombardo, and later raised by Giorgio Massari in 1755. Above the tower is an open terrace on which stands a bell with a figure on either side. The bell is sounded by the hammering of the two male figures that were cast in bronze by Ambrogio da le Anchore in 1496 and dubbed the Moors because of the dark coloring they have taken on as their metallic surfaces have weathered over the almost five hundred years they have been striking the hours in Venice. Beneath the terrace, is the winged lion, symbol of St. Mark the Evangelist and the city of Venice herself. Below the Lion is a jutting semi-circular balcony with a niche in the middle and a door on either side. The niche contains a gilded copper statue of the *Virgin and Child* which has been attributed to the sculptor and goldsmith Alessandro Leopardi who was born sometime in the second half of the 15th century and died 1522-1523. Each year on the feast-day of the Ascension (which comes 40 days after Easter) and during the whole time of Ascension week festivities, at the striking of every hour, figures of the Three Magi preceded by an angel, go in and out of the doors, pass in front of the Virgin, and bow before her. This charming tradition is still observed and is truly one of the most picturesque sights to be enjoyed during springtime in Venice. Below the semi-circular balcony is the huge face of the intricate clock works placed there at the end of the 15th century. It was created by two craftsmen, father and son, Giampaolo and Giancarlo Ranieri from Parma. It was restored in 1757 by B. Ferracina.

Piazza San Marco: the Procuratie Vecchie, the Procuratie Nuove and the Napoleonic Wing.

PROCURATIE VECCHIE – NAPOLEONIC WING – PROCURATIE NUOVE

Extending the length of the Clocktower side of the square is the building known as the **Procuratie Vecchie** which has fifty arches on the ground floor level and two upper floors of loggias. It was begun between the end of the 15th and first half of the 16th centuries by Mauro Coducci who designed the first floor. Following the fire of 1512, Bartolomeo and Guglielmo Grigi succeeded Coducci and added on the second storey, although the building was completed by Sansovino. The name «Procuratie Vecchie» (Old Magistrature) was given to distinguish the building from the «Procuratie Nuove» (New Magistrature) whose design is in keeping with the earlier building, so that the square an effect of stately harmony and balance. On the far side of the square, the side of San Gemignano, a very old church which Napoleon ordered torn down in 1807 so that a huge ballroom leading out of the royal palace (Palazzo Reale) could go up in its place, is the Ala Nuovissima (Most recent Wing) or the **Ala Napoleonica** (Napoleonic Wing). It is a neo-Classical design by Giuseppe Soli, who repeated the double orders of the Procuratie Nuove, adding to the top level a frieze of statues of Roman emperors and mythological and allegorical scenes. On the south side of the square is the **Procuratie Nuove**. Influenced by the Classical style of Sansovino's Library, Vincenzo Scamozzi designed it in 1584 and supervised the construction up to the tenth arch. The rest was once the residence of the *Procurators of St. Mark* but when the Republic fell in 1797 it was turned into the royal palace.

Today it is occupied by cultural institutes such as the Correr and Archeological Museums.

THE ARCHEOLOGICAL MUSEUM

An important collection of Classical art is laid out in twenty rooms of the Procuratie Nuove. Begun by Cardinal Domenico Grimani in 1523 and bequeathed by him to the Republic, it is made up of marble and bronze archeological finds from Rome and Greece.

Only the highlights of the twenty rooms will be indicated. Room I contains an extensive collection of Greek and Roman inscriptions, of special interest for scholars. Room 2 has four showcases in which a practically complete collection of Roman coins is on display. Room 3 offers some fine pieces of Greek sculpture including *Hecate* (3rd century B.C.), the *Sosandra Aphrodite* (15th century B.C.) and a *torso of Apollo*. Room 4 contains outstanding 5-4th century B.C. sculptures: the headless *Athena*, the *Grimani Hera*, and, in the center, the *Persephone* which dates from the time of Phidias. Room 5 contains Greek and Roman Classical works including *Dionysus and the Satyr* and the celebrated *Grimani Altar*. Room 7, of special note are the headless *Aphrodite*, the *funerary stele of Lysandra*, and the superb *Zulian cameo*, upon which the *Ephesus Jupiter with his aegis* is carved. Room 8 contains Hellenistic works such as the 3rd century B.C. *Ulysses*, a Roman copy of a Greek original. Room 9 has a fine collection of Roman portraits ranging from the Republican period to the 3rd century A.D.; those of Pompeus and Vitellius are especially fine. Room 10, Roman portraits continued. Room 11, shows Greek and Roman reliefs. In the showcases are ivories and small bronzes. Room 12, statues of Venus. Room 13, *Mithras sacrificing a bull*. Room 14, a series of finely-crafted vases. Room 15 contains a fascinating collection of Roman altars, reliefs, and plaques. Room 16 has various ancient statues restored or re-integrated in the XVIIth Cent. Rooms 17 and 18 display the Egyptian sculpture and Greek reliefs originally in the Correr collection. Room 19 contains a fine Roman sarcophagus and prehistoric artefacts, and Greek bronzes and ceramics in the showcases. Room 20, the Near East collection, has Egyptian mummies and Egyptian statuettes, and Assyrian reliefs in the showcases.

THE CORRER MUSEUM

The Museo Civico Correr occupies the so-called Napoleonic or «Nuovissima» wing (west side) and the Procuratie Nuove (south side). The entrance is from the arcade of the Napoleonic wing. The collection was begun in 1830 by a wealthy Venetian nobleman, Teodoro Correr, who bequeathed most of his collection to his native city. The museum remained in the Palazzo Correr on the Grand Canal until 1922 when it was moved to its present site. The collection was so big it had to be split up into different sections: one pertaining to 18th century Venice dispayed in the Palazzo Rezzonico, archeology in another wing of the Procuratie Nuove (entered from the Piazzetta), and those we are about to see, again broken up into three departments: History, Paintings, and 19th Century Italian History (*Il Risorgimento*).

The Historical Section – In the room leading to the Historical Section is a youthful masterpiece by Antonio Canova, a statue of *Dedalus and Icarus*; the neo-Classical decorative scheme is by G. Borsato. The museum, thirty-three rooms in all, contains a vast array of objects and furnishings relating to the history of Venice's institutions, art, and social changes. Among the highlights: the Lion of St. Mark's, flags and emblems of the Republic, portraits and emblems of doges, decrees issued by the doges, descriptions of magnificent public ceremonies, attire worn by doges and' high-ranking public officials, relics of the conspiracy led by Bajamonte Tiepolo, superb collections of coins, documents, drawings and paintings of naval formations, relics of the celebrated Battle of Lepanto, nautical maps and instruments, portraits of the great Venetian explorers and navigators and the great map of their colonial conquests, as well as fascinating weapons, emblems, flags, scepters, and trophies.

The Painting Gallery – This section consists of nineteen superbly decorated rooms on the third floor. For reasons of space we cannot list all the works on display; we shall mention just the highlights in each room. Room 1, the Venetian Byzantine school: in addition to some fine paintings, there is a stupendous 13th century dower chest known as the *Cassa di Beata Giuliana* which shows Blessed Giuliana with Sts. Biagio and Cataldo. Room 2, 14th century Venetian painting, features works by Paolo Veneziano. Room 3 contains works by Lorenzo Veneziano. Of special note is the panel showing *Christ giving the keys of the kingdom to St. Peter* which originally was part of an altarpiece. Room 4: the 14th century panel paintings of *Virtues* and the early 14th century statuette of *Doge Tommaso Mocenigo*, by Jacopo Dalle Masegne should not be overlooked. Room 5, Venetian High Gothic painting: of major interest are Stefano Veneziano's *Virgin enthroned* and, in the centre, a 14th century painted *Crucifix*. Room 6, Venetian High Gothic painting continued: a fine *Virgin and Child* by Jacobello del Fiore, and altarpiece with *scenes from the life of St. Mamante*, by Francesco dei Franceschi, and a *Virgin and Child* by Michele Giambono. Room 7, Cosmè Tura: displayed are masterpieces by the 15th century painter from Ferrara whose distinctive tormented style produced such remarkable paintings as this *Pietà*. Room 8, the Ferrarese School: there are other fine works by Ferrarese artists, as well as two superb *Virgins* by Bartolomeo Vivarini. Room 9, contains several Venetian wood sculptures. Room 10, the Flemish School paintings, including an *Adoration of the Magi* by Pieter Brueghel. Room 11: three extraordinary paintings are to be found here: Antonello da Messina's *Pietà* (second half of the 15th century) Hugo Van der Goes' *Crucifixion*, and Bouts' *Virgin and Child*. Room 12: among the Flemish and German masters displayed are Cranach, Bruyn, and Civetta. Room 13, the Bellinis. This family of artists dominated the whole Venetian art world from the end of the 15th to the beginning of the 16th century. Among the masterpieces of two generations of Bellinis here are Jacopo's *Crucifixion*, Gentile's *Portrait of Doge Giovanni Mocenigo* and Giovanni's *Transfiguration, Virgin and Child, Pietà* and a small *Crucifix-*

The Correr Museum: Virgin and Child, by Giovanni Bellini.

The Correr Museum: Portrait of Doge Giovanni Mocenigo, by Gentile Bellini; right: **the Courtesans, by Vittore Carpaccio** (detail).

ion. Room 14: Alvise Vivarini and his followers, featuring a superb *St. Anthony of Padua*. Room 15: Vittore Carpaccio's most famous painting, the *Courtesans*. Room 16: Carpaccio and followers of Bellini, including a fine *Portrait of a youth with a red beret*. Room 17, noteworthy are a *Virgin and Child* by Lorenzo Lotto, a *Bust of a youth* by Giovanni Dalmata, and a *Virgin and Child with saints* by Boccaccino. Room 18, the «*Madonneri*» (Greco-Venetian painters of the 16th and 17th centuries). Room 19: a collection of 16th century ceramics of incredible beauty and workmanship. The *Servizio Correr*, a service of seventeen pieces decorated by Niccolò Pellipario c. 1525, is particularly noteworthy.

The Risorgimento Museum – This 20-room section is devoted to relics of the period during which the Italians were struggling to attain their national identity and unity. It was set up after Venice was annexed to the Italian state under a bequest made by Piero Marsich, one of the main figures in the heroic but unsuccesful fight against the Austrians in 1848-1849. The rooms illustrate the fall of the Republic of Venice after a millenium of independence, the period of Napoleonic occupation, the Austrian domination, the conspiracies, the defense and surrender of the city in 1849 and finally, the liberation from the Austrians.

THE BELLTOWER

This is the oldest belltower in Venice, having been built over Roman foundations, starting from the time of Doge Pietro Tribuno (888-912) and then off and on over the years. Among the numerous artists who had a hand in it were Niccolò Barattieri and Bartolomeo Malfatto (the bell chamber), Proto Bon and Giorgio Spavento. For centuries it withstood the onslaught of storms and earthquakes. Then, at 10 am on July 14, 1902, weakened by centuries of vicissitudes and less than perfect workmanship, it suddenly collapsed, luckily without causing a single victim or

Sansovino's Loggetta; left: **the Belltower.**

damage to the nearby monuments (except for Sansovino's Logget-ta which was shattered into fragments and buried beneath the rubble). The loggia was put back piece by piece and the belltower itself was reconstructed exactly as it had been on the same spot. It was re-opened to the public on the feast-day of St. Mark, the patron to welcome back the «*paron de casa*» (master of the house) as the Venetians dubbed the building whose bell chamber commands a remarkable view over the whole city and the lagoon.

A convenient elevator will take you up to the bell chamber of the 320-foot tower. On top of the cusp is a gilded angel weathervane. When the tower collapsed in 1902, four of its five bells, the Angel, and the nearby Loggetta were all smashed to pieces, but they were put back together again thanks to the painstaking labor of a Venetian craftsman, Emanuele Munaretti.

The Loggetta – At the foot of the Belltower is the marvelous three-arched loggetta built by Sansovino between 1537 and 1549 to replace a 13th century one which, moved from the neighborhood of San Basso, had been set up here. In 1569 it housed the Armed Guard of the Republic when the Greater Council was in session. The four bronze statues in the niches of the façade depict *Apollo, Mercury, Pax* (Peace) and *Minerva*, each symbolizing an aspect of the Republic: Apollo, its power, Mercury, the eloquence of its ambassadors and intellectuals. Peace, supposed to inspire the Venetians' political activities and Minerva, the high-level attained in the arts, sciences, government, and war. The four statues are proof of the great skill that their creator, Sansovino himself, had achieved as sculptor in his mature period. The fine bronze gateway and putti on either side of the top are by Antonio Gai (1735). The allegorical reliefs (they allude to Venetian power) have been ascribed to Tiziano Minio and Danese Cattaneo.

Basilica of St. Mark's: the façade.

THE BASILICA OF ST. MARK'S

The cathedral of Venice grew together with the Sea Republic's rising power. In the year 828 the mortal remains of St. Mark the Evangelist were triumphantly borne to Venice and safety, far from the desecration supposedly intended by the Moslems of Alexandria of Egypt. Welcomed with solemn ceremonies and rites, the relics were at first placed in the Palace Chapel, actually the tiny Church of San Teodoro. But it was hardly worthy of the new-and now sole-patron saint of the *Serenissima Repubblica*, so Doge Giustiniano Partecipazio decided to remedy the situation by bequeathing a considerable sum of money for the building of a basilica befitting such valuable relics. His wish was carried out by his brother, Giovanni Partecipazio, who set about the huge task of erecting a church alongside the Doges' Palace in 829.

By 832 the building had all its main structures up and by 883 it was fully decorated. In 976, during an uprising of the Venetians against the despotic doge, Pietro Candiano IV, the Doges' Palace was set on fire and the flames also damaged the adjoining basilica, which was only restored years later by the canonized

40

The Basilica of St. Mark's with Piazzetta San Marco in the background.

doge, Pietro Orseolo. Then, shortly after the year 1000, Doge Domenico Contarini decided that the basilica was not as magnificent as the beautiful Romanesque churches being built in all the mainland cities and had it demolished. In its place he commissioned the church as we know it today. According to a number of reliable scholars, the grandiose project got underway in 1063, whereas others maintain that it was begun several years later and finished after Contarini's death. The plan chosen by the doge was wholly Byzantine, a Greek cross shape covered by a series of domes (although the treatment was more Romanesque than Byzantine), yet the name of the architect has not come down to us. In any case, the building was finished in 1073. Originally rather plain, if not austere-looking, St. Mark's was soon adorned with superb mosaics, precious marble from Roman Altinum, and various architectural and decorative elements from the Orient. For centuries, Venetian travelers, merchants, and admirals carted – off war spoils and souvenirs to donate to the great church, so that today St. Mark's is a complex yet harmonious combination of Byzantine, Gothic, Islamic and Renaissance elements.

When visiting the church, we recommend following the numbers in bold type in the text which refer to the plan on page 42.

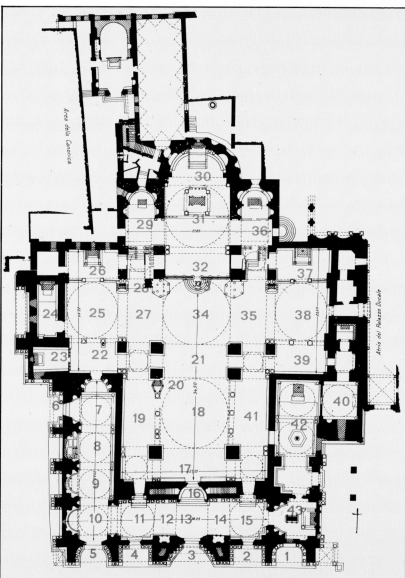

Plan of the Basilica of St. Mark's – **1.** First portal. **2.** Second portal. **3.** Center portal. **4.** Fourth portal. **5.** Portal of Sant'Alipio. **6.** Porta dei Fiori. **7-15.** Atrium. **16.** Church door. **17.** Arcone del Paradiso. **18.** Dome of the Pentecost. **19.** Left aisle. **20.** Capitello del Crocifisso. **21.** Great Western Arch. **22.** Portale della Madonna. **23.** Cappella dei Mascoli. **24.** Cappella di Sant'Isidoro. **25.** Dome of San Giovanni. **26.** Cappella della Madonna Nicopeia. **27.** Great Northern Arch. **28.** Crypt of St. Mark's. **29.** Cappella di San Pietro. **30.** Apse. **31.** Main altar. **32,** Great Eastern Arch. **33.** Pulpits. **34.** Dome of the Ascension. **35.** Great Southern Arch. **36.** Cappella di San Clemente. **37.** Altar of the Sacrament. **38.** Dome of San Leonardo. **39.** Right transept. **40.** Treasury. **41.** Right aisle. **42.** Baptistry **43.** Cappella Zen.

The Tetrarchs.

THE FAÇADE – Along its approximately 169 feet runs a porch of five rounded arches protruding into the square. A delicate marble railing separates the ground floor level from the upper one with the four famous **gilded bronze horses.**

The whole building, dominated by five Oriental domes, seems unreal, almost as if it were a stage set. Before taking a more detailed look at the façade, we shall stop to observe the south side of the façade (i.e., that closest to the Doges' Palace). On the corner is a porphyry sculptural group showing two pairs of male figures embracing. The famous sculpture, called «*the Tetrarchs*», is thought to be Syrian and most likely represents four emperors, namely Diocletian, Maximian, Galerius, and Constance. Nearby are two square *columns* which were brought here from St. John of Accra in Syria. On the upper section of the church is a Byzantine mosaic depicting the *Virgin*. One of the perpetually-lit lamps by it recalls the legend of the poor baker's boy unjustly executed for a crime he never

Above: **the Removal of the body of St. Mark**; below: **the Venetians, worshipping the body of St. Mark.**

committed. On the corner bordering the square is a truncated column, the «*pietra del bando*» (decree stone), which came from Syria. Here all the laws passed by the government were read aloud to the people assembled below. We shall now take a closer look at the five portals opening onto the square (starting from the right). In the first one (1) bearing elaborate Moorish decorative motifs is a mosaic showing the *Removal of St. Mark's body from Alexandria in Egypt*, a 17th century work by Pietro Vecchia. In the second one (2) is another mosaic by Vecchia of the *Arrival of St. Mark's body in Venice*. The central one (3) is adorned with fine Venetian Romanesque bas-reliefs depicting *Professions, Months*, and *Virtues*. Above the portal is a fine 12th century Romanesque sculpture of the *Angel appearing to St. Mark*. The mosaic above, representing, the *Last Judgment*, is a 19th century work after a design by Lattanzio Querena. The fourth portal (4) has a bronze door cast in the 14th century by Master Bertuccio. Above is a mosaic of the

Above: **the Deposition, the Resurrection;** below: **the Descent into Limbo, the Ascension.**

Body of St. Mark being worshipped by the Venetians by Sebastiano Ricci (1728). The fifth portal **(5)** is called the Portal of Sant'Alipo after the statue of the saint to be found here. It is adorned with columns, capitals, and reliefs of various origins, mainly Byzantine, removed from older church buildings. The mosaic, datable 1260-1270, and showing the *Venetians carrying the body of St. Mark into the church*, is especially fascinating because it allows us to see what St. Mark's looked like at the time. If you want a closer look at the works on the upper floor of the façade, you are allowed to walk out on the terrace from the galleries inside the church. However, to get a proper overall view of the façade, we recommend taking time out to walk back on the square far enough to embrace the whole with a single glance. Beneath the elegant marble terracing in between the arches are noteworthy 12th century Byzantine reliefs. From left to right, they portray: *Hercules and the wild boar, the Virgin, St. George, St.*

45

Piazzetta dei Leoncini.

Demetrius, the Archangel Gabriel, and Hercules and the doe. On the loggia above the main portal are the replicas of the four marvelous 4th century B.C. Greek **horses** that Enrico Dandolo brought to Venice from Constantinople in 1204. They were placed on this spot in 1250. (The originals have been carefully restored and can be seen inside the Museum of St. Mark's). Behind the horses are four 11th century eight-sided columns with fine carved capitals and the huge window of the central arch. The mosaics in the smaller arches on either side, based on cartoons by Maffeo da Verona, portray (from left to right): the *Deposition*, the *Descent into Limbo*, the *Resurrection*, and the *Ascension*. The elaborate sculptural decoration of the upper floor is one of the most remarkable sculptural compositions of the Italian Gothic period. Art historians believe that the project was begun by the Dalle Masegne family in 1385. Then, after a great fire in 1419, it was restored, continued, and altered by various Florentine and Lombard artists.

LEFT SIDE OF ST. MARK'S, PIAZZETTA DEI LEONCINI, AND PORTA DEI FIORI – On the north side of the church is the Piazzetta dei Leoncini (Square of the Little Lions) named after the two marble lions sculpted by Giovanni Bonazza in 1722. In front of the Porta dei Fiori (Flower Portal) are three arches surmounted by fine Gothic sculptures. In the center of the first arch is a symbolic representation of the 12 Apostles (12 lambs). Then, after a relief of *Alexander the Great carried up to Heaven*, a 10th century work, between the first and second arches, we find ourselves before the Porta dei Fiori. Unfortunately, nothing remains of the original construction, probably datable around 1200, the period when this side of the church was being remodelled. The Arab-Moorish style arch which has elaborate carvings of flowers and branches (and a lunette relief of a *Nativity*) gave the portal its name. After the fourth arch are five 12th and 13th century Byzantine reliefs in the protuberances, the finest of which

Basilica of St. Mark's: atrium.

shows *Christ blessing the four Evangelists*. Farther on, beneath an arch, is the **tomb of Daniele Manin** by Luigi Borro. Manin died in Paris in 1857 and his remains were brought to his native city in 1868. Facing into the Piazzetta is the Baroque façade of the suppressed **church of San Basso**, attributed to Giuseppe Benoni, and built c. 1670. In the center are marble fountains in the form of well-rings and on the far side is the **Palazzo Patriarcale** with a neo-Classical façade by Lorenzo Santi (1837-1850).

THE ATRIUM OF ST. MARK'S – In order to get the best possible view of the atrium, enter by way of the main portal. All aglow with a splendid mantle of golden mosaic, the atrium space is divided, by slightly pointed arches, into separate bays topped by hemispherical domes, except for the central one (by the portal through which we entered) which is open. Measuring 201x19 feet and almost 24 feet tall, the atrium has remained unchanged for seven hundred years. The pavement too is covered with mosaics that create incredible light effects when the church is flooded, as it often is, in fall and winter. The marble columns against the walls are of various origins, some are even said to have come from the Temple of Solomon in Jerusalem. Following the numbers on the map is the best way to look at the porch mosaics which recount stories from the Old and New Testaments. Practically all the mosaics were executed by Venetian masters who demonstrated incredible technical skill in their treatment of colour and form. Their lively narrative style is typical of the Romanesque period.

7 – The Porta di San Giovanni is to the left of the Porta dei Fiori. On the dome and lunette are *stories from the life of Moses* and, in the spandrels, figures of *Solomon, David, Zachariah,* and *Malachi*. Directly over the door is the *Virgin and Child between Sts. John and Mark*.

8 – The dome recess contains 17th century mosaics executed after designs by Pietro Vecchia showing *Sts. Apollinaire, Sigismund,* and *St. Francis with the Stigmata. Stories from the life of Joseph* (13th century) cover the dome, with the four Evangelists in the spandrels.

9 – The stories *from the life of Joseph* are continued. The tomb in the exedra belongs to Doge Marino Morosini who died in 1253.

10 – The mosaic in the semi-dome, executed in 1583 by Giuseppe Bianchini after a cartoon by Salviati, shows the *Judgment of Solomon*. The dome has *Stories from the Life of Joseph*, with four Hebrew prophets in the spandrels. All of these mosaics were done in 1240, but they underwent extensive restoration in the 19th century. An anonymous Pisan sculptor carved the Doge Bartolomeo Gradenigo's tomb (who died in 1342), which is visible in the exedra.

11 – The lunette of the Porta di San Pietro has a Byzantine mosaic of *St. Peter*. The dome and side lunette contain several *scenes from the life of Abraham* in the Romanesque-Byzantine style.

12 – the 13th century ceiling mosaic shows the *Drunkenness* and *Death of Noah,* the *Construction of the Tower of Babel,* and the *Lamentation of the multitudes*. The sepulchral wall contains the tomb of Felicita Michiel, wife of Doge Vitale Falier, who died in 1101.

13 – In the upper niches is a *Virgin with saints*, in the lower ones, *Apostle*. These works were done in the 12th century and were influenced by the Ravennate school. The bronze panel on the portal has figures of saints cast between 1112 and 1138. The mosaic in the semi-dome, by Valerio and Francesco Zuccato who executed it in 1545 after a design by Titian, depicts *St. Mark in ecstasy*. The same craftsmen also carried out the ceiling decoration (after designs by Pordenone) in 1549. The mosaics represent the *Resurrection of Lazarus,* the *Crucifixion,* the *Deposition,* and the *Death of the Virgin,* with *Evangelists and Prophets* in the spandrels. The red marble slab on the pavement marks the exact spot where the Emperor Frederick Redbeard fell to his knees before Pope Alexander III on July 23, 1177.

14 – Fifteen marvelous *Scenes from the Life of Noah* and the *Flood* decorate the inside of the archway. On the outside is the niche tomb of Doge Vitale Falier who died in 1096.

15 – The bronze panels of the Porta San Clemente are divided into 28 rectangular compartments, each bearing a figure of a saint, beneath which is a Greek inscription in silver (a Byzantine work executed in Constantinople). In the lunette is another mosaic by Valerio Zuccato,

Atrium of the Basilica: Stories of Noah and the Flood.

dated 1532, of St. Clement. The three-part dome is decorated with mosaics dated c. 1230. They represent various episodes of Genesis, from the *Creation of Heavens and Earth* and the *Creation of Adam and Eve*, up to the story of *Cain and Abel.*

16 – The main entrance to the church. On the left is a door leading to the upper galleries and the museum.

INTERIOR OF THE CHURCH – What makes the interior of the church so striking is the unusual combination of simple architectural forms and an incomparable wealth of decorative motifs. The plan of the building: a Greek cross, with three aisles for each arm of the cross. Five huge domes sustained by massive pillars crown the whole while the arcades which run all the way round the basilica are supported by rare marble columns with gilded capitals, mostly Byzantine in character. The patterned flooring made of coloured marble dates from the 12th century. Its unevenness is due to the shifting of the structure which rests on pylons. The church including the vestibule, is c. 249 feet long and c. 203 feet at the crossing; the center dome is c. 139 feet on the outside, and c. 91 on the inside. The Doge supposedly told the unknown architect about to start work on the project that it should be the most beautiful building ever built. And so it was – a vision of 4000 sqms of glittery gilding and mosaics upon gold ground. The mosaic work was carried out by Venetian craftsmen in various periods. Noteworthy was the contribution of great Renaissance masters from Tuscany. The whole decorative scheme pivots around the theme of the

Basilica of St. Mark's: inside view.

glorification of the Church of the Saviour. It would be practically impossibile to describe all the mosaics, sculpture, and architectural elements in St. Mark's, so we shall proceed only with a description of the highlights. However, we recommend going to the upper galleries to get the best view of the mosaics.

17 – Above the center portal is a 14th century mosaic of *Christ blessing* *between the Virgin and St. Mark*. In the arch above is a grandiose mosaic of the *Apocalypse according to St. John* by Pordenone and Zuccato (1570-1589) Behind the Apocalypse, against the center window, is the **Arcone del Paradiso (Arch of Paradise)** with scenes of the *Last Judgment* executed in the 16th and 17th centuries. Major artists such as Jacopo Tintoretto. Antonio Vassillacchi, Maffeo da Verona, and Domenico Tintoretto contributed to the huge undertaking.

18 – The Pentecost Dome – In the center is the white dove symbolizing the Holy Spirit whose divine breath spreads out in the form of tongues of fire over the seated Apostles. Between the tiny arched windows are representations of the nations of Christendom and, in the spandrels, monumental *Angels*. These mosaics date from the first half of the 12th century.

19 – Left aisle – The mosaics depict *Christ and Four Prophets* (13th century). among the precious marbles adorning the wall are *Paradise* and the *Triumph of the Trinity* by G. Pilotti and the *Martyrdom of Apostles Peter and Paul* by Palma the Younger and Padovanino. The right arch contains the *Crucifixion of St. Andrew* by Aliense and the *Murder of St. Thomas* by Tizianello, the left one the *Miracles of St. John* by Patavino. These mosaics all date from the 17th century.

20 – Capitello del Crocifisso – This is a hexagonal shrine of six precious marble columns surmounted by carved Byzantine capitals. Inside is a panel painting showing a Crucifixion which probably came from Constantinople. According to a legend, it supposedly bled when a maniac attacked it with a knife.

21 – The Great Western Arch – The 12th century mosaic decoration has a dramatic rendition of *Scenes of the Passion*. The episodes are shown in five separate compartments. The dramatic *Crucifixion* scenes are especially noteworthy.

22 – On the ceiling and wall are fine mosaics with scenes of the *Life of the Virgin* and the *Childhood of Christ*. The ceiling mosaics date from the 13th-14th centuries, those on the wall are 16th century works. Jacopo Tintoretto and Palma the Younger took part in the project.

23 – Cappella dei Mascoli – Founded in 1430, it got its name in 1618 when it belonged to an all male religious confraternity. The sculptures have been ascribed to the Bon family. The fine mosaics, executed between 1430 and 1450, show *Scenes from the Life of the Virgin*. The two lefthand episodes are by Michele Giambono and the *Visitation* and the *Death of the Virgin* on the right were executed after cartoons by J. Bellini and A. Mantegna.

24 – Cappella di Sant'Isidoro – The chapel was commissioned by Doge Andrea Dandolo between 1354 and 1355 to contain the mortal remains of St. Isidore which have been placed on the altar in a Venetian-Gothic sculpted urn. The 14th century mosaics covering the walls and ceiling show fifteen episodes from the life of St. Isidore rendered in a lively narrative style.

25 – The Dome of St. John – It is adorned with 13th century mosaics in the Venetian-Gothic syle showing Romanesque influence. The mosaics portray *Scenes from the Life of St. John* with *four saints* in the spandrels. Two of the saints, *Sts. Gregory* and *Jerome*, are by Giambattista Piazzetta.

26 – Cappella della Madonna Nicopeia – Before entering the chapel, do not overlook the *Altar of St. Paul*, an exquisite Renaissance sculpture against the lefthand pillar. The carved altar frontal showing the *Con-*

Western Arch: the Crucifixion.

version of St. Paul has been attributed to Pietro Lombardo. The statue of St. Paul on the altar is in the style of Lombardo. The chapel contains the image of the *Madonna Nicopeia* (the Virgin of Victories) which is greatly venerated by the Venetians who consider her their protectress. The image, actually a Byzantine painting with Oriental enameling predating the year 1000, was brought to Venice from Constantinople by Doge Enrico Dandolo in 1204. The altar is by Tommaso Contino (1617), while the sculptures of the *Virgin and Saints* are Venetian-Gothic works of the 11th and 12th centuries. The decorative mosaics beneath the arches were added in the 17th century.

27 – The Great Northern Arch – The mosaics represent the *Wedding at Cana* and *Supper in the house of Simon* (after cartoons by Jacopo Tintoretto), *Christ healing the leper* by P. Veronese, and the *Healing of the sick man* and the *Resurrection of the son of the window Naim* by Giuseppe Salviati. In the small arch are *Four Prophets*.

St. Luke and St. Mark, the Evangelists.

28 – The Crypt of St. Mark's – The crypt, beneath the choir, reached by a flight of stairs, has ribbed vaults upon Greek and Byzantine columns. The mortal remains of St. Mark were laid to rest here in 1094, but were later removed since the crypt, lying below the lagoon water level, was subject to periodic flooding. After extensive alteration, it was completely dried out and reopened to the cult in 1889.

29 – Cappella di San Pietro – Before the actual chapel is an «iconostasis» (rood screen) with five sculpted saints attributed to the school of the Dalle Masegne family. The relief of St. Peter on the smaller altar is a 14th century Venetian school work. The mosaics covering the walls portray *Scenes from the Lives of Sts. Mark and Peter* (2nd half of the 13th century). A door behind the altar of St. Peter leads to the sacristy, while the one on the lefthand side leads to the church of San Teodoro. The lovely **Sacristy** with its mosaic ceiling was built in 1486. The *Christ* in the center of the ceiling is probably by Titian, the four *Evangelists* around him and several figures of

53

St. Mathew and St. John, the Evangelists.

Apostles in the lunette of the righthand wall have been attributed to Lorenzo Lotto, and, in the recess of the portal, the figure of *God the Father* is by Padovanino. On either side of the portal are *two figures of St. Jerome*, pieces submitted to a competition held in 1563, by Domenico Bianchini known as «*Il Rosso*» (The Redhead) and his nephew, Giannantonio. The inlays on the three finely-executed cabinets portray *Scenes from the Life of St. Mark, Still-Lifes, and Landscapes.* Although crafted by several different artist, they seem to have an overall compositional pattern inspired by a single master whose style recalls Vittore Carpaccio's and, in fact, art historians believe that the extraordinary panels were based on Carpaccio cartoons. The **Chiesetta di San Teodoro**, now part of the sacristy, is Renaissance in style. In the past it was the headquarters of the Inquisition Court. Over the altar are sculptures by Sansovino and, on the wall, a mosaic of *St. John the Almsgiver* by Pietro Vecchia. To the left of the altar is the entrance to the *Aula Capitolare* (Chapter Room) containing a number of noteworthy paintings such as the *Adoration of the Shepherds* by

G. B. Tiepolo and portraits of confraternity directors by followers of Gentile Bellini, Titian, B. Strozzi, and P. Longhi (whose altarpiece portraying *St. Lorenzo Giustinian and an Altarboy* is especially interesting).

30 – The Apse – The apse is entered through the Cappella di San Pietro. The Byzantine mosaics between the windows, untouched by the fire of 1106, are the oldest in St. Mark's. They represent *Sts. Nicholas, Peter, Mark,* and *Hermagoras*. The door leading to the sacristy is by Sansovino.

31 – The Main Altar and Choir Dome – The main altar is surmounted by a tribune resting upon four precious columns made of Oriental albaster and covered with reliefs depicting *Scenes from the Lives of Christ and Mary* sculpted by 13th century Venetian masters. Above are statues of the *Saviour* and the four *Evangelists*. To the left of the Ciborium are four bronze sculptures representing the *Evangelists* by Sansovino and the four statues opposite them are the *Fathers of the Church* sculpted by Girolamo Pagliari in 1614. Inside the main altar are the relics of the Evangelist Mark, while over it is the celebrated masterpiece of medieval goldsmithing, the **Pala d'Oro**, by the Venetian master Giampaolo Boninsegna (1345). 10 feet long and almost 5 feet tall, it was originally commissioned from artists in Constantinople in 978, then embellished in 1105 with gold and enamels brought to Venice after the Fourth Crusade, of 1204 from the Monastery of the Pantocrator. Boninsegna is also responsible for the embossing and for setting the gemstones. The Golden Altar-piece has eighty enamel plaques which illustrate *Scenes from the Lives of Christ, the Virgin, and St. Mark*, as well as figures of angels, prophets, the Evangelists, and Oriental emperors. The choir dome is covered with a *mosaic of Christ Pantocrator* (Christ blessing), the *Virgin and Prophets*, with the figures of the *Evangelists* in the spandrels.

32 – The Great Eastern Arch – Opposite the main altar is an impressive rood screen. This consists of a coloured marble railing on top of which eight columns support an architrave with statues of *St. Mark*, the *Virgin*, and the *Apostles*. The fourteen statues are by Jacobello and Pier Paolo Dalle Masegne (1394). The bronze and silver *Crucifix* in the center is by Jacopo and Marco Bennato. On either side of the choir are elaborate inlaid stalls crafted by a Jesuit monk, Fra Vincenzo, and four lecterns decorated with bronzes by Sansovino. In the overhead arch are mosaics with New Testament scenes of the *Life of Christ* executed after cartoons by Jacopo Tintoretto.

33 – On either side of the rood screen are two ambos (pulpits). On the left is the so-called **double ambo** dating from the 14th century: the lower one, for readings from the Epistles, is an eight-sided structure resting on eleven columns made of precious marbles, while the upper one, for readings from the Gospel, rests upon seven columns and is covered with a gilded bronze dome. The ambo on the right is known as the **Pulpito della Reliquia** since on major feast-days relics of the saints were shown from it. Here the newly-elected Doge was presented to the people. The statue of the *Virgin* above has been attributed to Giovanni Bon.

34 – The Dome of the Ascension – It is decorated with a 13th century Byzantine mosaic in which Western influence can be felt. The mosaic shows *Christ in Glory* surrounded by fluttering angels with the Virgin and apostles assembled below. Between the windows are personifications of the sixteen *Virtues* that were essential characteristics of the living Christ. Figures of the *Evangelists* and the four *Sacred Rivers* mentioned in the Bible adorn the spandrels.

The Golden Altar Screen and detail of the great Christ Pantocrator; top right: incense burner from the treasure vault of St. Mark's.

35 – The Great Southern Arch – The subjects of these superb 13th century mosaics are *Jesus entering Jerusalem*, the *Temptation of Christ*, the *Last Supper*, and the *Washing of the feet*. *God the Father in Glory* in the center is a 17th century work by Giacomo Pasterini.

36 – Cappella di San Clemente – This chapel, like the choir, is preceded by a red marble rood screen. Four columns support an architrave adorned with statues sculpted by the Dalle Masegnes in 1397. The relief on the altar depicting the *Virgin* is by Pirgotele (1465). The Doge could attend Mass without being seen by listening at the barred window to the right of the altar. On the left is a reliquary also sculpted by the Dalle Masegnes. The scenes illustrated in the ceiling are the *Removal of the body of St. Mark from Alexandria*, the *Departure from Egypt*, and the *Arrival in Venice*. The mosaics beyond the organ with *Scenes from the Life of St. Clement* date from the 13th century.

37 – The Altar of the Sacrament – In front of the altar is a pair of bronze candlesticks by Maffeo Olivieri (1527). On the right is a 15th century relief depicting *St. Peter amidst the worshippers* and, on the left, a Byzantine *Virgin*. Against a column is an *Angel* in front of which burns an eternal light in memory of the prodigious discovery of the body of St. Mark. The mosaics in the arch depict the *Parables* and *Miracles of Christ*, whereas those covering the wall above the altar and between the windows illustrate *Scenes from the Life of St. Leonard* to whom the altar had originally been dedicated. Pietro Vecchia is the author of the mosaics.

38 – The Dome of St. Leonard – These 13th century mosaics contain images of several saints greatly venerated by the Venetians: *Sts. Leonard, Nicholas, Blaise* and *Tecla* by Vincenzo Bastiani (1512). Under the small inner arch are other 15th mosaics with *Figures of Saints*. On the outer one around the Gothic rose-window dating from the 15th century are fine mosaics narrating the *Miracles of Christ* by G. Pauletti. The Doge entered the church through the door beneath the rose-window.

39 – The right transept – At the far side is the entrance to the Treasury. Over the door is a 13th century Moorish arch. In a lunette between two mosaic *Angels* is a 14th century *Ecce Homo*. Underneath the lefthand arches are mosaic renderings of *Sts. Geminian* and *Severus*.

40 – Treasure-vault of St. Mark's – Before the treasure-vault is the so-called «Sanctuary» which has a collection of 110 reliquaries as well as other sacred fittings. The Treasury contains the relics and precious artefacts that the Venetians acquired over the centuries through trade or as war booty.

41 – The right aisle – The right wall is covered with superb Venetian school mosaics showing both Byzantine and Romanesque influence. They represent the *Virgin in prayer* and *Four Prophets* (1230). Beneath the last arch is a huge holy water font composed of a basin carved out of a single piece of porphyry and decorated with sculptures by the Lombardos.

42 – The Baptistry – The Venetians call it «*Chiesa dei Putti*» (Church of the Babies), since here infants (putti) are baptized. Doge Andrea Dandolo (who is buried here) commissioned it in 1350. The huge baptismal font was designed by Jacopo Sansovino and beautifully crafted by Desiderio Fiorentino, Tiziano Minio, and Francesco Segala. The bronze lid is decorated with figures of *Evangelists* and *Scenes from the Life of St. John the Baptist*. The statuette of *St. John the Baptist* is also by Segala (1575). Before the altar is the tomb of one of the greatest Venetians, Jacopo Sansovino. A gilded silver 13th and 14th century Byzantine relief behind the altar portraying the *Baptism of Christ* and *Sts. George* and *Theodore*. Here too the ceilings, lunettes, and domes are adorned with 14th century mosaics. The finest of these are *Christ and the Apostles preaching the Gospel* and the *Banquet of Herod* (on the dome), *Christ in Glory amidst the heavenly hosts* (on the dome above the altar) and scenes from the life of *St. John the Baptist* and the *Crucifixion* (on the lunettes and walls).

43 – The Cappella Zen – The Republic decreed the erection of this superb chapel in memory of Cardinal G. Battista Zen who, before he died in 1501, bequeathed a rich legacy to his native city. The cardinal's tomb in the center was cast in bronze by Paolo Savin. The other sculptures and bronzes are by Savin and others (Pietro Campanato, A. Leonardi, and A. Lombardo). On the bronze altar is a statue, also in bronze, known as the «*Virgin of the Shoe*», since, according to a legend, a shoe donated to the image by a poor man miraculously turned into solid gold. The 14th century

The Baptistery.

mosaics recount the *Life of St. Mark*. In the apse semi-dome is the *Virgin and Child with angels*, while on the wall is a Byzantine relief, with a Greek inscription, of another *Virgin*. In Lombard-style niches are lovely statuettes of four *Prophets* and a superb Venetian-Romanesque *Nativity*.

Retracing our steps, we return to the atrium where we climb the stairs to the **MARCIANO MUSEUM** which has a superb collection of tapestries, rugs, old lace, and other works of art. The highlights are: the four beautifully restored **Gilded Bronze Horses**, the replicas of which have replaced them on the balcony above the main entrance of the basilica, the organ panels by Gentile Bellini, ten tapestries with scenes from the *Passion of Christ* (after designs by Zannino di Pietro), four tapestries with *Stories from the Life of St. Mark* (executed in 1551 after designs by Sansovino), and an *altarpiece* by Paolo Veneziano dated 1345. One of Veneziano's masterpieces, the altarpiece once served as the cover for the Pala d'Oro on the main altar and has *Scenes from the Life of St. Mark*, the *Dead Christ*, and the *Virgin and Saints*.

View of the Ducal Palace from the quay.

THE DOGES' PALACE

The name of the architect who designed this remarkable building has not come down to us, but whoever it was made it the symbol of the supreme power and glory of the Republic of St. Mark's. It was on this site that, towards the end of the 9th century, Doges Angelo and Giustiniano Partecipazio established the seat of the government which came to be known as the «Palazzo Ducale» (Doges' Palace), since it was the residence of the Doge, the supreme head of state. However, the impressive structure we see today retains nothing of its 9th century origins. In fact, before the year 1000, when it was a Byzantine palace built over pre-existing Roman walls, the 9th cent. building was gutted in a fire.
Thereafter it was rebuilt a number of times, until 1340, when it assumed its present-day form. Actually, tradition ascribes the building of the 14th century palace to Filippo Calendario, stone-cutter, Pietro Baseio, and Master Enrico. The façade facing the lagoon was completed during the years 1400-1404, whereas the Piazzetta side was not ready until 1424. Although renowned masters from Florence and Lombardy were called in to take part in decorating the prestigious building, most of the ornamental design in the elaborate Flamboyant Gothic style was handled by a Venetian family of artists, who were highly skilled marble crafts-men, the Bons. The result is this incredible building, seemingly

Ducal Palace: detail of the balcony.

suspended over the double tier of arcading which gives it such a dainty airy effect. Then in 1577 another fire broke out, burning down an entire wing. Another competition for its reconstruction was announced and entries from the most celebrated architects of the day poured in. The project submitted by Antonio Da Ponte, architect of the Rialto Bridge, was selected and the building was restored to its 14th century appearance.

THE FAÇADES – A person approaching the palace from the canal is confronted with a light-distilled vision, seemingly hovering weightless in mid-air with delicate pink and white patterned walls. The façade is symmetrically divided by the lovely carved balcony built by Pier Paolo and Jacobello Dalle Masegne in true Flamboyant Gothic style (that is, with elaborate sculptural decoration). Rising above the whole is a statue of Venice clad as Justice, a 16th century work by Alessandro Vittoria.

Above: **the Accra pillars;** right: **Porta della Carta.**

Worthy of attention amongst the elegant carved capitals of the arcade columns is the first one on the Piazzetta side representing *Adam and Eve in the Earthly Paradise* (early 15th century). The west façade facing the Piazzetta closely resembles the south (canal) side, with a balcony erected by pupils of Sansovino in 1536 imitating the one designed by the Dalle Masegnes. Over the pointed arch window is a panel with Doge Andrea Gritti before the symbol of Venice, a modern work by Ugo Bottasso, and, on the very top, a statue of Justice by Alessandro Vittoria. Right by the façade of the church of St. Mark's on the Piazzetta side is the so-called **Porta della Carta**, literally the Charter Portal, to which government decrees were affixed. It was originally known as the «golden portal», since it was once decorated in blue and gold. The upper section, elaborately carved as befits the Flamboyant Gothic taste, is the work of the Bon family. Just above the doorway is a statue of *Doge Foscari kneeling before the Winged Lion* (modern), while the topmost enthroned figure represents Justice. On the corner of the Doges' Palace is a famous sculptural group depicting the *Judgment of Solomon*. This 15th century sculpture has been variously attributed to either Pietro Lamberti or Nanni di Bartolo.

THE INTERIOR – Now that the damage caused by the popular uprising of 1797 at the time of the French occupation has been repaired, the interior of the Doges' Palace and all of the art masterpieces it contains have been restored to their former splendour. Here, for hundreds of years, the Doges and high-ranking officials of the Republic vied in accumulating extraordinary pieces to adorn these rooms in which the most important decisions regarding the life of the city were deliberated.

I NORMANNI
POPOLO D'EUROPA MXXX · MCC

28 MAGGIO - 19 SETTEMBRE
TUTTI I GIORNI

Ducal Palace: the courtyard.

The Courtyard – The Porta della Carta brings us to the **Foscari Portico** which we cross to enter the courtyard of the Doges' Palace. Its effect is at the same time peaceful and majestic. In the middle is a pair of imposing bronze well-rings. The one closer to the portal is by Alfonso Alberghetti (1559), while the other is by Niccolò del Conti (1556), both of whom worked as cannon forgers for the Republic of St. Mark's. The main or eastern façade (facing the entrance) was designed by Antonio Rizzo at the end of the 15th century. Its pleasing aesthetic effect is largely a result of the harmony of the architectural elements achieved by combining the lower Gothic section with the upper Renaissance level. If you think about it, such bold blending of different styles is a hallmark of Venetian architecture and underlies its special charm. The elaborate decorative scheme is by Pietro Lombardo (15th century). The right side was designed by Scarpagnino in the mid 1500s, whereas the two brick façades which border the courtyard on the south and west sides were built by Bartolomeo Manopola in the 17th century as imitations of the outer façades. The arches of the north façade, on top of which is a giant clock, are separated from each other by niches with restored antique statues inside them, another Baroque creation by Manopola. To the right, set on a tall base, is a monument to Francesco Maria I della Rovere, Duke of Urbino, sculpted by Giovanni Bandini in 1587. By the Staircase of the Giants is the **Foscari Arch**, begun by the Bons in the Gothic style, and later finished by Rizzo and the Bregnos according to the Renaissance taste. Along the top of the structure are Statues of St. Mark and other allegorical figures. The niches below contain *statues of Adam and Eve*, bronze copies of Antonio Rizzo's originals now inside the palace. Alongside the Staircase of the Giants is

Ducal Palace: the Giant's Staircase.

the tiny **Courtyard of the Senators** where the senators of th Republic supposedly assembled during official ceremonies. The **Staircase of the Giants** received its name from the two colossal statues of *Mars* and *Neptune* on either side of the landing. The statues are by Sansovino and his pupils; the overall project, however, was designed by Antonio Rizzo at the end of the 15th century. On the landing at the top of the stairs the new doges were officially crowned. Having climbed the staircase we are on the second floor loggia.

THE SECOND FLOOR (OR PIANO NOBILE) – To reach the upper floors of the palace we take the **Scala d'Oro**, literally, the Golden Staircase, designed by Sansovino in 1538 for Doge Andrea Gritti, but completed by Scarpagnino in 1559. The staircase, with a barrel vault ceiling covered with splendid gilded stucco reliefs, was originally reserved for the VIPs of the day. The first arch at the entrance is decorated with two sculptures by Tiziano Aspetti (2nd half of the 16th century) portraying *Hercules and Atlas*. Two statues by Francesco Segala symbolizing *Abundance and Charity* decorate the third floor. The second floor, which served as the doges' private apartments, was first occupied by Doge Agostino Barbarigo towards the end of the 15th century, as it had to be completely rebuilt after the 1483 fire.

Sala degli Scarlatti (the Scarlet Room) – The room received its name from the scarlet-coloured togas of the high-ranking members of the doge's entourage who foregathered here. The splendid ceiling decoration of a gold pattern against a blue ground was executed by Biagio and Pietro da Faenza in 1505. The Lombardos sculpted the carved fireplace on which you

Ducal Palace: the Grimani Room; left: **the Golden Staircase.**

˙can see the coat-of arms of the Barbarigo family. The stucco relief depicting the *Virgin and Child* is a Paduan school work. Opposite is a relief representing *Doge Leonardo Loredan presented to the Virgin by St. Mark*, in a style reminiscent of Pietro Lombardo.

Sala dello Scudo (the Shield Room) – The shield belonging to Venice's last doge was preserved here, hence the room's name. In addition, it once served as an assembly hall for the doge's private guards. The maps around it were made in 1762 by F. Grisellini who based himself on existing maps made prior to 1540.

Sala Grimani (the Grimani Room) – In the center of the ceiling is the coat-of-arms of the Grimani family after whom the room was named. The

Ducal Palace: the Room of the Four Doors.

painted frieze just below the ceiling which has been attributed to Andrea Vicentino consists of panels with allegorical scenes. The marble fireplace was sculpted at the beginning of the 16th century by Tullio and Antonio Lombardo.

Sala Erizzo (the Erizzo Room) – On the fireplace is the coat-of-arms of Doge Erizzo. The carved ceiling dates from the 16th century. From the adjoining terrace, transformed into a hanging garden, there is a fine view over the courtyard.

Sala degli Stucchi (the Stucco Room) · The stucco decoration dates from the time of the dogeship of Marino Grimani. Several interesting paintings hang here: an *Adoration of the Magi* by Bonifacio de' Pitati, a *Portrait of Henry III* by Tintoretto, an *Adoration of the Shepherds* by Leandro Bassano, and a *Holy Family* by Salviati.

Sala dei Filosofi (the Philosophers' Room) - Twelve portraits of philosophers by Veronese and Tintoretto, now in Sansovino's Library, used to hang here. A long corridor leads to the *doge's private chapel* whose door is adorned with an image of *St. Christopher*, a fine work by Titian.

The Painting Collection - These three rooms, once belonging to the doge's private suite, overlook the little canal behind the Doge's Palace. Noteworthy are the 15th century fireplaces with the Barbarigo coat-of-arms, set into elaborate decorative schemes. In the rooms are paintings once hung elsewhere in the palace. The first one contains a *Lamentation* by Giovanni Bellini and, facing it, Carpaccio's famous *Lion of St. Mark's* painted in 1516, which has an interesting view of the harbor of St. Mark's in the background. In the second room are paintings by the famous 16th century Flemish painter, Bosch. The two panel paintings represent Heaven and Hell, while the subjects of the two altarpieces are the *Temptation of Sts. Jerome, Anthony and Egidius* and the *Martyrdom of St. Juliana*. These paintings called «*stregozzi*» (literally, spellbinders) are typical products of Bosch's striking imaginative genius. In the third room is a *Virgin and Child* by Boccaccino and a *Lamentation* by Antonello da Saliba.

Sala degli Scudieri (the Squires' Room) - This room is reached through the Map Room. The fine works on display include *Venice receiving the homage of Neptune* by Tiepolo, the *Annunciation* by Palma the Younger, and three allegorical paintings by Domenico Tintoretto.

THE THIRD FLOOR - We retrace our steps to the Scala d'Oro and go up a flight. The third floor occupies the whole east wing of the building and was rebuilt over a long period after being destroyed by fire.

Atrio Quadrato (the Square Atrium) - The octagonal painting in the center of the carved wooden ceiling of *Doge Gerolamo Priuli receiving the sword and scales from Justice* by Tintoretto shows the master's skill at achieving striking compositional and colouristic effects. Two of the several noteworthy paintings displayed here are *Adam and Eve* and the *Prayer in the Garden*, both by Paolo Veronese.

Sala delle Quattro Porte (the Room of the Four Doors) - This was once the assembly hall of the Collegio (Council), but it later served as a special antechamber to the Senate Hall. Built by Antonio Da Ponte after a design by Andrea Palladio, it has elaborate gold and white stucco decoration. The subjects of the paintings are allegorical representations of the power and glory of the Venetian republic. Of special note are the allegorical ceiling frescos by Tintoretto and the celebrated painting of *Doge Antonio Grimani Kneeling before Faith in the presence of St. Mark* by Titian.

Anticollegio (the Antechamber) - People waiting to be received by the doge assembled here. On the ceiling is *Venice distributing honors and rewards* by Veronese. The elaborate fireplace was designed by Vincenzo Scamozzi. Four masterpieces by Tintoretto adorn the walls: *Vulcan's forge, Mercury and the three Graces, Bacchus and Ariadne*, and *Minerva dismissing Mars*. Veronese painted the much-restored *Rape of Europa*.

Sala del Collegio (the Council Hall) - This is where the doge and the highranking magistrates held audiences and discussed affairs of state. The room was designed by Palladio and built by Da Ponte. On the ceiling

Ducal Palace: Senate Room.

is a superb cycle of paintings by Veronese whose skillful treatment of light and harmonious compositional patterns create particularly attractive effects. The subjects of these allegorical paintings are the *Allegory of Faith* (center), *Sacrifice* (below), *Venice enthroned crowned by Justice and Peace* (above the tribune), *Mars and Neptune* (above the entrance), and a series of allegorical figures. On the tribune wall is the *Glorification of the Victory of Lepanto* by Veronese, while paintings by Jacopo Tintoretto complete the decorative scheme.

Sala del Senato (the Senate Hall) - Here the doge presided over the senate meetings. The subjects of the paintings are all related to the glorification of Venice and her rulers. On the ceiling is Tintoretto's *Venice, Queen of the Seas* and, over the doge's throne, two other Tintorettos, the *Dead Christ* and *Doge Loredan praying to the Virgin to end the famine and concede a victory over the Turks*. Above the door opposite the throne is a painting by Palma the Younger depicting *Doges Lorenzo and Girolamo Priuli praying to the Saviour to end the plague*.

Antichiesetta (the Chapel Antechamber) - The ceiling of this stuccoed room has frescoes by Guarana representing *Allegories of Good Government*. On the walls are the cartoons done by Sebastiano Ricci for the façade of St. Mark's, showing the *Arrival of the Body of St. Mark in Venice*.

Chiesetta (the Chapel) - It was built by Vincenzo Scamozzi in 1593. On the altar is a sculpture of the *Virgin and Child with St. John* by Jacopo Sansovino and on the ceiling are frescoes by Guarana.

Sala del Consiglio dei Dieci (the Hall of the Council of Ten) - In this room the much-feared Ten (magistrates) who watched over the security of the state held their meetings. The subjects of the paintings all pertain to the

Ducal Palace: Room of the Council of Ten.

council's functions. In the center of the ceiling is a copy of a Veronese, *Jupiter smiting Vices*. The original, carried off by the French in 1797, is now in the Louvre. The *Old man in Eastern dress with a girl* and *Juno offers the doge's hat to Venice* are by Veronese.

Sala della Bussola (the Booth Room) - The «booth» is actually the double door leading to the adjoining Sala dei Capi del Consiglio dei Dieci. Here people about to be questioned and the condemned were kept waiting. Along one of the walls you can still see the notorious «*bocche di leone*» (literally, lions' mouths), actually slots into which anonymous citizens could drop denunciations. The fireplace is by Sansovino and his helpers. On the ceiling is a copy of a Veronese, *St. Mark and the Virtues*, the original of which is in the Louvre.

Sala dei Tre Capi del Consiglio dei Dieci (the Room of the Three Heads of the Council of Ten) - Of special note are two paintings by Veronese, the *Punishment of the Forger* and *Sin vanquished by Victory*, and the fireplace by Jacopo Sansovino.

Saletta degli Inquisitori (the Inquisitor's Room) - In this room (which is in direct communication with the prisons) people were brought in front of the Inquisition for questioning. The ceiling paintings are by Tintoretto.

The Landing of the Scala dei Censori - Retracing our steps through the Sala della Bussola we come out by the staircase leading up to the Weapons Rooms.

The Sale d'Armi del Consiglio dei Dieci (the Weapons Rooms of the Council of Ten) - In the past, these rooms were used as prisons, but starting from the early 14th century, they were turned into armouries.

Ducal Palace: Room of the Booth.

Today they contain a fascinating, easy-to-follow collection of weapons of the past. The objects on display cover swords (one of which is an especially fine example of 14th century Venetian craftsmanship), pikes, halberds, armour (including the armor worn by Henry IV King of France and two suits of armour that once belonged to the Sforza family), and a twenty-barrel arquebus. Among the sculptures are a *marble bust of Sebastiano Venier*, the hero of the Battle of Lepanto, by Alessandro Vittoria, a *bronze bust of Francesco Morosini* by the Genoese artist Filiberto Parodi, and a *bronze bust of Marcantonio Bragadin* by Tiziano Aspetti.

We return, by way of the **Scala dei Censori**, to the second floor (where we have already visited the doge's private apartments). We shall now tour the remaining rooms.

Andito del Maggior Consiglio (the Corridor of the Great Council) · This hallway overlooking the harbor is illuminated by beautiful Gothic windows. On the right wall are works by Palma the Younger, on the left, works by Tintoretto.

Ducal Palace: Armoury.

Sala della Quarantia Civil Vecchia (the Room of the Forty) - This room was the seat of the Supreme Court composed of forty members. It too is adorned with allegorical and commemorative paintings.

Sala del Guariento (the Guariento Room) - Originally it was called the Armaments Room as ammunition was stored here, but now it contains what is left of a masterpiece, the *Paradise* fresco by the 14th century Paduan artist, Guarinetto, which was originally painted for the Sala del Maggior Consiglio. Damaged in the fire of 1577, it was replaced by a painting of the same subject commissioned from Jacopo Tintoretto in 1580. We can appreciate its great beauty from this *Coronation of the Virgin*, peopled with figures of angels, saints, and prophets.

Sala del Maggior Consiglio (the Hall of the Greater Council) - This incredibly huge hall (it measures 177 feet long, 82 feet wide, and 50 feet high) was used for meetings of the Greater Council, the Republic's governing body. Five huge Gothic windows looking out on the harbor, two on the Piazzetta, and two on the courtyard afford splendid views over the

Ducal Palace: Hall of the Great Council.

lagoon and all the famous sights in the vicinity. After the 1577 fire which
destroyed the original hall that had been officially inaugurated by Doge
Francesco Foscari in 1423, it was soon rebuilt by Antonio Da Ponte with
decorations based on the iconographic ideas of a Florentine scholar,
Girolamo de' Bardi and the Venetian historian, F. Sansovino. Upon
entering you are immediately struck by the huge painting above the
tribune (measuring 72x22 feet). It represents *Paradise* and was painted by
Tintoretto between 1588 and 1590. Although numerous restorations have
marred a good deal of the original light and shade contrasts, nothing can

harm the impressive monumentality of the compositional pattern. Christ and the Virgin are surrounded by saints disposed in ever-widening circles on a multiplicity of perspective planes. The overwhelming ceiling composed of thirty-five compartments set in grandiose gilded frames was built by Cristoforo Sorte between 1578 and 1584. Turning our backs to the platform, we shall now examine the highlights of the ceiling paintings, starting from the ones by the harbor wall and then passing to the right side and back to the Door of the Quarantia Civil Nova. 1 - *Antonio Loredan commands the attack to free Scutari from the siege of Mohammed II*, by Paolo Veronese. 2 - *The Venetian army and navy conquer Polesella*, by Francesco Bassano. 3 - *Vittore Soranzo and his fleet victorious at Argenta* (1482) *against the troops of Ercole I d'Este*, by Jacopo Tintoretto and his helpers. 4 - *Jacopo Marcello's conquest of Gallipoli* (1494), by Tintoretto. 5 - *Giorgio Cornaro and Bartolo defeating the imperial troops of Maximilian I at Cadore*, by Francesco Bassano. 6 - *Andrea Gritti reconquering Padua*, by Palma the Younger. 7 - In the oval, *Venice crowned by Victory welcomes the vanquished peoples and conquered provinces*, by Palma the Younger. 8 - In the main panel. *Venice surrounded by sea divinities hands an olive branch to Doge Niccolò Da Ponte*, by Tintoretto. 9 - In the oval, *Apotheosis of Venice*, by Veronese. 10 (courtyard side) - *Pietro Mocenigo leading the Venetians to victory at Castelmaggiore*, by Francesco Bassano. 11 - *Stefano Contarini defeating the Visconti navy at Riva in 1440*, by Tintoretto. 12 - *The Venetians led by Francesco Barbaro helping the city of Brescia break the siege of Filippo Maria Visconti*, by Tintoretto. 13 - *Carmagnola leading the Venetians to victory at Maclodio in 1426*, by Francesco Bassano. 14 - *Francesco Bembo leading the Po fleet to victory over Visconti's troops in Cremona*, by Palma the Younger. The *Portraits of Doges* just beneath the ceiling are by Domenico Tintoretto and his helpers. There is also an empty space covered by a black cloth with a Latin inscription that reads: «This is the place of Marin Faliero, beheaded for his crimes» (high treason). The subjects of the paintings along the courtyard wall are related to the struggle between Pope Alexander III and Frederick Redbeard in which Venice was politically involved. The most interesting are the *Ambassadors petitioning Redbeard for peace* by followers of Tintoretto (fourth panel from the far side of the room), the *Pope handing a sword to the doge* (fifth panel), and *Frederick Redbeard prostrate before the Pope* by Federico Zuccari (tenth panel). Paintings of scenes of the IVth Crusade against the wall overlooking the quay. *A Portrait of Doge Contarini after the victory of Chioggia*, by Veronese on the wall opposite the *Paradise* wall.

Sala della Quarantia Civil Nuova (New Room of the Civil Court Forty) - This was the seat of the appeals court for citizens residing on the mainland. The fine gilded beam ceiling dates from the 1500s. Above the tribune, partially lined with gilded leather, on which the various judges' coats-of-arms have been embossed, is a 15th century *Virgin* against a gold ground. The paintings along the walls represent *Venice and Justice* by A. Foler, *Venice and Neptune*, the *Virtues*, and *Justice expelling the Vices* by G. B. Lorenzetti, and *Justice and Time strip Truth naked* by F. Zaniberti.

Sala dello Scrutinio (the Voting Room) - Starting in 1532, this room was where ballots were cast for the election of the Greater Council and where commissioners for the election of the doge met. Before the 1577 fire its walls were adorned with paintings by Tintoretto and Pordenone. After being restored by Antonio Da Ponte in 1587, the great hall was redecorated. The theme of the paintings commissioned was once more the glorification of Venice's triumphs on the high seas, drawn up by erudite scholars. Again, not being able to list each and every work, we shall give

only the highlights. In the elaborate gilded ceiling attributed to Sorte is the *Conquest of Padua* by Francesco Bassano, on the entrance wall the *Last Judgment* by Palma the Younger, on the courtyard wall the *Battle of Lepanto*, by Andrea Vicentino. Beneath the ceiling are portraits of doges, a continuation of the series started in the Sala del Maggior Consiglio. The balcony affords a splendid view over the Piazzetta and the church of St. Mark's. At the far end of the room is a grandiose *Triumphal Arch*.

Sala della Quarantia Criminal (the Room of the Criminal Court Forty) - Reached from the Scala dei Censori, the room contains a noteworthy *Lion of St. Mark's* by Jacobello del Fiore.

Sala del Magistrato al Criminal and Sala del Magistrato alle Leggi - (the Room of the Criminal Court Magistrate and the Room of the Law Magistrate) - Antonio Rizzo's original marble sculptures *Adam* and *Eve* (1470), once in the Foscari Arch of the courtyard, have been placed here.

The Prisons - By the Scala d'Oro, on the east side of the Loggias, is a small door which leads to the prisons and the Bridge of Sighs (see p. 82), which communicated with the *Avogaria* (magistrates' office) and other courts. Through the Bridge of Sights prisoners were led before their judges. Prior to the construction of the *Palazzo delle Prigioni* (Prison Building), this was known as the Old Prison. It was composed of two sections: the *Piombi* (literally, lead) whose cells were located under a lead roof and the *Pozzi* (wells), dank and dark dungeons below the level of the lagoon in which the most dangerous criminals were kept. The eighteen cells making up the *pozzi* may be visited by descending a flight of stairs.

We shall now visit the suite of rooms known as the *Avogaria* in the east wing of the Doges's Palace on the same floor as the loggias.

Sala dei Censori (the Room of the Censors) - The room served as offices for the two *censori* whose job it was to watch over the behaviour of the nobles and denounce cheating in elections. Around the walls are the coats-of-arms of 266 *censori* (from 1517 to 1629) and portraits of several of them by Tintoretto and Palma.

Sala dei Notai or Sala dell'Avogaria (the Room of the Notaries or Advocates) - The walls are hung with portraits of famous *notai* and *avogadori* and several religious scenes by Leandro Bassano and Tintoretto's followers. On one of the walls hangs an odd clock with only six hours shown on its face. The *Avogaria* was in charge of the so-called Gold and Silver Books, kept in the adjoining Sala dello Scrigno, which listed the noble families of the city.

Sala della Milizia da Mar (the Room of the Militia of the Sea) - This was the headquarters for the captains in charge of recruiting men for the fleet of the *Serenissima*. The walls are decorated with 18th century frescoes in Tiepolo's style, one of which, the *Adoration of the Magi* has been attributed to Gian Domenico Tiepolo himself. A small adjoining room once served as the office of the *Segretario alle voci* (literally, Secretary of the Items) who was in charge of recording the names of those awarded public office.

Sala della Cancelleria Ducale (the Doges' Chancellery) - This room, where the Collegio dei Notai held its meetings, was the office of the Head Chancellor. From here a staircase descends to the *pozzi* which we have previously described.

Ducal Palace: Sala dello Scrutinio (Voting Room).

Ducal Palace: Entrance to the Prisons; below: **one of the "Pozzi"
(Wells).**

Ponte della Paglia (Straw bridge).

Museo dell'Opera di Palazzo (the Doges' Palace Museum) - The ground floor museum is well worth a visit. Exhibited here are the original capitals from the palace's outside colonnade, many of which had to be replaced for restoration, as well as columns, reliefs, several original pieces of crenellation, and the original architrave from the Porta della Carta by Bartolomeo Bon.

As soon as our tour of the Doges' Palace is over, we return to the Piazzetta and, turning left, walk down to the docks where we enjoy a glorious view of the harbor. To the left, along the southern side of the Palace, we come to the **Ponte della Paglia** (Straw Bridge), perhaps nicknamed for the barges transporting straw for the prisons which docked here. It was built in 1360 and then enlarged in the 19th century. On one of the pylons, facing outwards, is an image of the gondoleers' protectress, *Our Lady of the Gondoleers*, set inside a 16th century tabernacle.

Bridge of Sighs.

THE BRIDGE OF SIGHS

From the side of the Ponte della Paglia you are looking straight at the famous covered bridge, Ponte dei Sospiri, which connects the Doges' Palace and the Prigioni Nuove. Commissioned by Doge Marino Grimani, it was built by Antonio Contini at the turn of the 17th century in the typical Baroque style of the day. The name «Bridge of Sighs» presumbly derives from the sighs of the prisoners who had to cross it as they were being taken before the Inquisitors.

Riva degli Schiavoni.

RIVA DEGLI SCHIAVONI

A walk down the Riva degli Schiavoni from the Ponte della Paglia along the **Canale di San Marco** (St. Mark's Canal) to the Giardini di Castello (Castle Gardens) is one of the Venetians' favorites. The Riva was once the mooring station for trading vessels coming from Slavonic ports (present-day Dalmatia). Originally no wider than the Ponte della Paglia, it was paved in 1324 and then widened in 1780. Running approximately a third of a mile, today it is a pleasant promenade filled with famous hotels and cafés.

MUSEUMS AND GALLERIES

The Academy Galleries: façade of the Museum.

THE ACADEMY GALLERIES

Five hundred years of Venetian art are on show in the Accademia which, for homogenity, clarity of exposition, and quality, cannot be equalled anywhere. Its origins go back to 1750 when the Republic of St. Mark's decided to endow the city with an «*Accademia di Pittori e Scultori*» (Academy of Painters and Sculptors) under the direction of Piazzetta. The original Academy occupied the Fondachetto delle Farine (Flour Storehouse), today the Port Authority, situated by the gardens of the former Royal Palace overlooking the harbor of St. Mark's. In 1756 the Academy was granted official recognition and Piazzetta, by then an old man, decided to leave it in the capable hands of Giovan Battista

Tiepolo. This was when the core of the first group of works by the pupils of the Academy was assembled. In 1807, during the French occupation, it was decided to transfer the art school and the works displayed in it to a more fitting place and the choice fell upon the *Scuola* and Church of the Carità (in the Campo della Carità) and upon the former monastery of the Lateran Canons, a building designed by Palladio in 1560 (but greatly altered since then). The collection thereafter considerably expanded as numerous works from suppressed churches and monasteries continuously poured in. During the period 1816-1856 bequests from Molin, Contarini, Venier, and Manfrin brought in new treasures. Lastly, several works returned from Austria after the San Germano Treaty was signed in 1919, and still other outstanding works were purchased by the Italian State. Somebody always asks why the name of the museum is Academy Galleries in the plural, even though there is only a single museum. Actually, the museum originally had two separate sections, one for paintings and the other for plaster casts used by the art students and the plural name has remained.

ROOM 1 - This splendid room is reached by a monumental staircase built in 1765 and adorned with two fine allegorical statues by Morlaiter. The stupendous gilded carved ceiling frames paintings by Alvise Vivarini and Campagnola. The room is devoted to 14th and 15th century Venetian school paintings. Of special note is the impressive altarpiece by Paolo Veneziano, still full of Byzantine influence. The subjects of the panels are the *Coronation of the Virgin and Scenes from the Lives of Christ and St. Francis*. Other fine works include the *Coronation of the Virgin* and *Justice between the Archangels Michael and Gabriel* by Jacobello del Fiore (1438) and the *Mystic Marriage of St. Catherine*, plus a superb altarpiece with the *Annunciation, saints, and prophets* by Lorenzo Veneziano.

ROOM 2 - The late 15th-early 16th century Venetian school. Several of the masterpieces of Giovanni Bellini, renowned for his skillful use of color and feeling for the mystical, are in the Academy collection. These include the *Sacra Conversazione* (originally in the church of San Giobbe) and the *Lamentation*. The *Presentation at the Temple* and *Crucifixion of the 10,000 martyrs on Mount Ararat* are by Carpaccio.

ROOM 3 - Cima da Conegliano and Giorgione. The *Female nude* painted by Giorgione in 1508 is unfortunately in very poor condition.

ROOM 4 - The major works are a *Virgin and Child with Sts. Paul and George, a Virgin and Child with Sts. Catherine and Mary Magdalene*, and a *Virgin with sleeping Babe* by Giovanni Bellini, the *Virgin of the Zodiac* by Cosmè Tura, and *St. Jerome* by Piero della Francesca (c. 1450). The *St. George* by Mantegna, despite its tiny size, conveys a great sense of monumentality and physical strength.

ROOM 5 - This room contains Giorgione's splendid much-discussed painting of the *Tempest*, full of symbolism and bathed in an atmosphere of lyrical melancholy. In addition, there are several more superb Bellinis including the *Madonna degli Alberelli*, the *Pietà*, and the *Virgin and Child with St. John the Baptist and a female saint*.

ROOM 6 - Paris Bordone painted the *Presentation of the Ring to the Doge*, which recounts a miracle of St. Mark, against a splendid background

The Academy Galleries: the Pietà, by Giovanni Bellini; left: St. George, by Andrea Mantegna.

showing 16th century Venetian life. Other important works are the *Banquet of the Rich Epulone* by Bonifacio de' Pitati, *St. John the Baptist* by Titian, and the *Madonna dei Tesorieri* by Jacopo Tintoretto (1566).

ROOM 7 - Lorenzo Lotto's *Portrait of a gentleman* reveals the painter's penetrating insight into the sitter's personality. Savoldo painted *St. Anthony Abbot with St. Paul the Hermit.*

ROOM 8 - Titian might have had a hand in this *Sacra Conversazione* regarded as Palma the Elder's masterpiece (1525). Also of note are Bonifacio de' Pitati's *Slaughter of the Innocents* and Romanino's *Pietà.*

ROOM 9 - Titian's school. The most interesting works are *God the Father blessing Venice* and the *Virgin and Child with Saints* by Bonifacio de' Pitati. The *Evangelists' symbols* are from Titian's workshop.

ROOM 10 - The 16th century Venetian school. This room contains several of the museum's major works from the height of the Venetian Renaissance. On of the most striking is the *Banquet in the House of Levi* which Paolo Veronese painted in 1573. The painter had intended this elaborate picture to represent the *Last Supper*, but the Inquisition Court, decreeing that the setting and poses of some of the figures were unbefitting to such a serious subject, compelled him to change the title. The *Miracle of the Slave*, painted by Tintoretto in 1548, was originally part of a whole cycle on the miracles of St. Mark. This work is a splendid example of Tintoretto's skill in using dynamic compositional patterns, emphasized by dramatic treatment of light and shade, which made him one of the greatest of the 16th century Venetian masters. The *Pietà* by Titian, commissioned for the church of the Frari, was the last work the master painted before his death.

The Academy Galleries: Madonna and Child, known as "Madonna degli Alberelli", by Giovanni Bellini.

ROOM 11 - The room is divided into two sections. In the first are *Adam and Eve*, the *Creation of the Animals*, and *Cain and Abel* by Tintoretto, and the *Mystic Marriage of St. Catherine* by Veronese. In the second are 16th and 17th century works by painters such as Tiepolo, Luca Giordano, and Pietro da Cortona.

ROOM 12 - The 17th century Venetian school. The highlights include several *Landscapes* by Marco Ricci, the *Rape of Europa* by Zuccarelli, and *Landscapes* by Giuseppe Zais.

The Academy Galleries: the Tempest, by Giorgione (detail).

ROOM 13 - The most interesting paintings are the *Rest on the flight to Egypt* and the *Virgin in Glory with St. Jerome* by Jacopo Bassano, the *Virgin and Child and Four Senators* and three *Portraits of Procuratori (magistrates)* by Tintoretto, and *Deucalion and Pirra, Christ and Pilate*, and the *Presentation at the Temple* by Schiavone.

ROOM 14 - Noteworthy are several canvases by Domenico Feti, including *David, Girl reading, Meditation*, and *Isaac and Jacob*. Jan Liss painted the *Sleeping Turk*, the *Sacrifice of Isaac*, and *Apollo and Marsyas*.

The Academy Galleries: detail from the Stories of St. Ursula, by Vittore Carpaccio (the Arrival of the Ambassadors).

ROOM 15 - 18th century works by Giovan Battista Tiepolo, Francesco Solimena, and others.

ROOM 16 - In addition to superb Tiepolos, this room also contains the *Fortuneteller* by Piazzetta, one of the best-known Venetian genre painters of the 18th century.

ROOM 17 - Antonio Canale, better known as Canaletto, is the foremost painter of the Venetian school called «*vedutismo*» (views). His pictures, painted in a crystal clear, terse style, appear as mirror-like reflections of reality. Paintings of his favorire subject, views of Venice, are spread throughout European museums. In this room is a *View of Venice* dating from 1765. The other renowned «*vedutista*» is Francesco Guardi, although his style stressing broad brushstrokes and a warm palette differs greatly from Canaletto's. Guardi is represented here with a *View of the Island of San Giorgio*. The delightful genre scenes of everyday life in 18th century Venice are by Pietro Longhi (the *Dancing lesson*, the *Concert*, the *Toilette*) and Rosalba Carriera (*Selfportraits*, the *French lady*, and *Portrait of a Youth*). The room also contains a series of attractive drawings by Sebastiano Ricci, Piazzetta, and Giambattista Pittoni.

ROOM 18 - 18th century paintings and sculptures. Of special interest are two sculptures, *Apollo* and *Wrestlers*, which are Antonio Canova's pieces when, at the age of eighteen, he applied for admission to the Accademia Art School, and a *St. Joseph with Child and saints* painted by Giovan Battista Tiepolo.

ROOM 19 - We return to the 15th century. The splendid *Flagellated Christ* is by Antonello da Saliba.

The Academy Galleries: Processions in Piazza San Marco, by
Giovanni Bellini.

ROOM 20 - Mostly paintings by Gentile Bellini, Giovanni's brother.
Influenced by Mantegna, Gentile loved huge compositions illustrating the
magnificence of Venetian public life in the 15th century: the *Procession in
Piazza San Marco* (1496) is not only a fascinating historical document but
an outstanding work of art as well. The *Miraculous healing of a possessed
man* by Vittore Carpaccio reveals the master's extraordinary narrative
skill.

ROOM 21 - Wall-size paintings which are part of a cycle on the theme of
the *Legend of St. Ursula* painted by Carpaccio from 1490 to 1496 for the
Scuola di Sant'Orsola which was suppressed at the time of the French
occupation in the late 1790s. The story of Ursula, the virgin princess from
Brittany, martyred during the Huns' siege of Cologne, is narrated in
Carpaccio's inimitable style, combining fanciful flights of imagination with
careful observation of down-to-earth everyday details.

ROOM 22 - We cross this early 19th century neo-Classical room on our way
back to Room 18 from which we enter the huge hall which was once the
upper part of the former church of Santa Maria della Carità.

ROOM 23 - This room features more 15th century paintings. The highlights
include Giovanni Bellini's four *Triptychs*, Carlo Crivelli's *Four Saints*, and
an altarpiece by Bartolomeo Vivarini depicting the *Nativity, Pietà and
angels and saints*.

ROOM 24 - Originally the pilgrims' lodgings of the Scuola della Carità, this
room has an impressive gilded carved ceiling. The outstanding work on
display is undoubtedly Titian's *Presentation at the Temple*. This famous
work was painted in 1538 when Titian had reached full artistic maturity.

XVIIIth CENTURY VENICE MUSEUM

The Museum is inside the Palazzo Rezzonico overlooking the Grand Canal. The palace, originally belonging to a noble Venetian family, Rezzonico, was the last home of Robert Browning. The City of Venice purchased it in 1935 and used it to reconstruct the interior of an 18th Century patrician dwelling.

A visit to the museum is the best way to get an idea of what Venice was actually like in the fascinating 1700s, the period so wittily recounted in Carlo Goldoni's plays and in Pietro Longhi's charming canvases.

From the atrium we take the monumental staircase up to the second floor. The first room we see is the huge Ballroom adorned with magnificent furniture carved by Brustolon. We then enter the Sala dell'Allegoria Nuziale (Room of the Nuptial Allegory) which was named after Tiepolo's painting of the *Marriage of Ludovico Rezzonico*. The Sala dei Pastelli (Pastel Room) contains several of Rosalba Carriera's delicate works. In the Sala degli Arazzi (Tapestry Room) are splendid Flemish tapestries. The Sala del Trono (Throne Room), originally the nuptial chamber, has a fresco in the middle by Tiepolo and, due to the splendor and magnificence of its furnishings, is one of the most elaborate in the palace. The Sala del Tiepolo (Tiepolo Room) is adorned with an allegorical fresco by Francesco Maffei. The Sala dei Lazzarini received its name from the two impressive paintings by the Lazzarini adorning it. The Sala del Brustolon features the Venetian master-craftsman's exquisite carved furniture and a sculpture collection. Third floor: The *Portego dei Dipinti* (Picture Hall) contains a collection of 18th century Venetian school paintings, including Piazzetta's *Selfportrait* and *Death of Darius*, Jan Liss' *Judith and Holofernes*, and several *Landscapes* by Giuseppe Zais. The Sala del Longhi (Longhi Room) contains 34 fascinating genre scenes of 18th century Venetian life by Pietro Longhi. The ceiling painting of *Zephyr and Flora* is by Tiepolo. After passing through two rooms frescoed by Guardi, we enter a delightful reconstruction of an 18th century Venetian bedroom. Two little rooms lead to another reconstruction, this one a re-creation of the Villa dei Tiepolo (Tiepolo Mansion) in Zianigo. These frescoes, all of which originally adorned the villa, are by Domenico Tiepolo, son of Giovan Battista. Of interest as well are the Camera dei Pagliacci (Clown Room), the chapel (frescoed by young Tiepolo in 1749), and the not-to-be-missed Sala del Ridotto which contains two renowned paintings by Guardi: the *Convent parlor* and the *Sala del Ridotto*. On the fourth floor is a reconstruction of an old Venetian pharmacy and a marionette theater.

THE FRANCHETTI GALLERY

The palace, along with its furnishings and an extensive collection of paintings of various periods and schools, was donated to the

The Museum of XVIIIth century Venice: Venetian chinoiserie lacquered chest of drawers.

Franchetti Gallery: Piazzetta di San Marco, by Francesco Guardi.

Italian state by Baron Giorgio Franchetti in 1916 and opened to the public in 1927. Nevertheless, none of the works or rooms bear identification plates or labels in accordance with Baron Franchetti's wish that it retain the appearance of a collection in a private home rather than take on the anonymous look of a state museum.

We shall list only the most important of the many important works in the collection. In order to make it easier for you to see the gallery, we have used numeration for the rooms which, as was previously mentioned, have deliberately been kept numberless and unlabeled. In the center of the splendid arcaded courtyard adorned with Roman and Greek sculpture is a fine 15th century marble well-ring. By the brick wall, a staircase resting on pointed arches leads up to the second floor loggia, or gallery, along which tapestries and sculpture are displayed. In the first room are two works by Carpaccio, the *Annunciation* and the *Death of the Virgin*, originally from the Scuola degli Albanesi, and an altarpiece with the *Passion of Christ* by Antonio Vivarini. In the second room is a *Sleeping Venus* by Paris Bordone. In the third, a *Bust of Benedetto Manzini* by Vittoria. The fourth room contains one of the museum's finest works, *Venus at her mirror* by

Titian. Another masterpiece hangs in the sixth room. *St. Sebastian* by Mantegna. In the seventh room on the third floor is a handsome *Portrait of a Gentleman* by Van Dyck. In the ninth room the two outstanding works are Pontormo's *Portrait of a Girl* and Filippo Lippi's *Nativity*. Among the many fine works in the tenth room we shall mention two lovely *Landscapes* by Francesco Guardi, the *Flagellation* by Luca Signorelli, and a noteworthy 15th century *Crucifixion* attributed to Jan Van Eyck. In the eleventh room are several Tintoretto portraits and other masterpieces of 16th century painting. From the third floor we may enter the remaining rooms of the gallery, which are actually part of the adjoining **Palazzo Giusti**: three of them contain Venetian school bronzes and Dutch and Flemish paintings.

THE QUERINI-STAMPALIA MUSEUM

The Querini Palace, which also houses the *Venice Public Library*, is located right behind the church of Santa Maria Formosa on Calle Querini. The picture gallery, featuring Venetian masters from the 14th-18th centuries, occupies twenty rooms on the second floor. The collection also includes rare furniture, china, arms and armour, as well as musical instruments.

Room 1 contains curious paintings of life in Venice by Gabriele Bella. Room 2, the *Coronation of the Virgin* by Catarino and Donato Veneziano. Room 3, portraits by Sebastiano Bombelli. Room 4, works by Palma the Younger, including *Adam and Eve* and a *Self-portrait*. Rooms 6 and 7, works by Venetian Mannerists, including *Landscapes* by Matteo de' Pitocchi. Rooms 8 and 9, the Renaissance. The highlights here are the *Adoration of the Virgin* by Lorenzo di Credi, *Sacra Conversazione*, by Palma the Elder, the *Virgin and Child* and *Presentation at the Temple*, by Giovanni Bellini, and *Judith* by Vincenzo Catena. Rooms 11-13, works by Pietro Longhi including the *Seven Sacraments, Hunt in the Valley*, and other genre paintings. Room 14, Marco Ricci's *Landscapes*. Room 15 through 20, drawings by Giovanni Bellini, Titian, Raphael, Tintoretto, Veronese, and other masters, in addition to Flemish tapestries wall hangings, objets d'art, weapons, ceramics, and Louis XVI lacquered furniture. Room 18, *portrait of G. Querini* by G. Battista Tiepolo. Room 20, *Virgin and Child* by Bernardo Strozzi.

THE GALLERY OF MODERN ART

Founded in 1897, the collection has steadily expanded as works from the famous Venice Biennial Art Exhibition have been added to it. The paintings and sculpture displayed range from the 19th and 20th century Venetian schools to a remarkable group of Italian and non-Italian contemporary masters.

International Gallery of Modern Art: the Troubadour, by
Giorgio De Chirico.

Among the many noteworthy artists we shall cite just a handful: Medardo
Rosso (the *Concièrge*, the *Laughing Lady, Mrs. Noblet*) Giorgio Morandi,
Zandomeneghi, Arturo Martini, Manzù (*the Great Cardinal*) Emilio Greco
(*Head of a lady*), Francesco Hayez (*Self-portrait*), Telemaco Signorini
(*November*), Giovanni Fattori, Auguste Rodin (*the Bronze Age*), Kandinsky,
Klee, Klimt (*Salomè*) Henry Moore, Savinio, De Chirico, De Pisis and a host
of others.

MAIN CHURCHES

The Church of Santa Maria Gloriosa dei Frari.

SANTA MARIA GLORIOSA DEI FRARI

This Romanesque-Gothic style Franciscan church, like its Dominican counterpart San Zanipolo, contains the tombs of a number of famous Venetian figures. Begun by the Franciscan monks in 1250, after a design attributed to Nicola Pisano, it was later re-elaborated and enlarged by Scipione Bon in 1338, though it was not finished until 1443. The stark façade is divided into three sections by pilaster strips surmounted by pinnacles. The statues over the central portal are by Alessandro Vittoria (1581). The Romanesque belltower is the second tallest in Venice, coming right after St. Mark's.

THE INTERIOR · The Latin cross interior, with three aisles divided by twelve plain columns, is truly majestic in its Franciscan simplicity. The church contains funerary monuments of numerous famous Venetians of the 14th to 18th centuries, not the least of which is Titian's. Right aisle: the first altar by Longhena was sculptured by Giusto le Court; second bay, the

97

The Church of Santa Maria Gloriosa dei Frari: the interior, with Assumption of the Virgin, celebrated altarpiece by Titian.

tomb of Titian, who died of plague in 1576, is a mediocre work executed by followers of Canova in 1852; third altar, sculptures by Alessandro Vittoria, among which a fine *St. Jerome*. To the right of the righthand transept is the monument to Jacopo Marcello, the Venetian admiral, by Pietro Lombardo. In the sacristy · which looks like a beautiful miniature church · is a masterpiece by Giovanni Bellini, still in its original frame, on the altar. The triptych painted in 1488 depicts the *Virgin enthroned, music-making angels, and saints*. In the third apse chapel is another triptych, this one by Bartolomeo Vivarini. On the altar of the first chapel is a statue of *St. John the Baptist* by Donatello. The choir: on the right wall is the Gothic-Renaissance monument to Doge Francesco Foscari by the Bregno brothers (c. 1475). On the left wall, a Renaissance masterpiece, the monument to Doge Nicolò Tron by Antonio Rizzo (1476). Behind the main altar is Titian's celebrated altarpiece, the *Assumption of the Virgin* of 1518, regarded as one of the greatest compositional feats in art history. In the first apse chapel on the left is a fine altarpiece by Bernardo Licinio (1535) in the third one, an altarpiece by Alvise Vivarini and Marco Basaiti representing *St. Ambrose enthroned* (1503). In the fourth chapel is a *triptych* by Bartolomeo Vivarini on the altar and on the baptismal font, a statue of *St. John the Baptist* by Sansovino (1554). Left aisle: over the second altar, the *Pesaro Altarpiece*, depicting the *Virgin with members of the Pesaro family*, by Titian (1526). Farther on is the *tomb of Antonio Canova* built from a design left by the great sculptor himself.

SANTA MARIA DI NAZARETH

The Church of Santa Maria di Nazareth.

Baldassarre Longhena was commissioned by the Barefoot (*scalzi*) Carmelite monks to design the church in 1670, but it was not finished until 1705, the year it was also consecrated. The façade, an outstanding example of the Venetian Baroque, was designed by Giuseppe Sardi, who drew his inspiration from Classical architecture. It consists of two tiers of twin columns framing huge niches which contain statues presumably carved by Bernardino Falcone. The whole is surmounted by a triangular tympanum adorned with sculpture. Unfortunately, one of the church's prize artworks, a fresco portraying The Transportation from the house of Loreto, by Giovan Battista Tiepolo, was destroyed during World War I. It has since been replaced by another fresco, *The Proclamation of the Motherhood of the Virgin at the Council of Ephesus*, by the painter Ettore Tito.

THE INTERIOR · The elaborate decoration of the aisleless interior perfectly reflects the rich decoration of the exterior. The inside is a profusion of sculpture, gilded stuccos, and colored marbles. The main altar, crowned by a canopy resting on eight marble columns, was designed by Giuseppe Pozzo in the exuberant Baroque style of the day. The statues of *St. Teresa and St. John of the Cross* on either side of the right is a ceiling fresco by Giovan Battista Tiepolo depicting *St. Theresa in Glory*. Another Tiepolo ceiling fresco is to be found in the first chapel on the left. It represents the *Sermon in the Garden* and the *Angel of the Passion*. In the second chapel on the left, known as the Cappella del Carmine, is the tomb of Ludovico Manin, the last doge of the Serenissima Repubblica di San Marco who ceased being doge on May 12, 1797 when the French overthrew the Republic.

SANTA MARIA DELLA SALUTE

The vicissitudes throughout the construction of the church were many and varied: here we shall try to recount the most interesting ones. In 1630 Venice was struck by a terrible plague which caused thousands to perish. The Senate thus deliberated that, should Divine Providence intercede on the city's behalf, the citizenry would erect a huge church in honor of the Virgin. The plague was overcome and the Senate announced a competition for the design of the church. All the outstanding architects of the day took part and the project was awarded to a young man, Baldassarre Longhena. Work began in 1631, but soon grave difficulties set in. First of all, the area was unable to support the weight of the building going up and the ground began to subside. Longhena solved the problem by inserting a host of supporting beams deep into the soil. But his troubles were not yet over. When the central dome was about to be set up, it looked as though the walls, would be unable to bear its weight. Longhena thought up an ingenious solution: he added a series of curlicue braces to help support the drum upon which the dome rests which, in fact, give the church its unique and distinctive appearance. By the time the church was consecrated in 1687, Baldassare Longhena had died five years earlier. Ever since, on November 21st each year, a picturesque procession, in which the whole city of Venice takes part, is held. On this occasion, a bridge connecting the church to the opposite shore is put up. The church has an octagonal plan and is surmounted by a great dome and a smaller dome directly over the choir.

The Church of Santa Maria della Salute.

THE INTERIOR · At the first righthand altars are paintings by Luca Giordano: the *Presentation of Virgin at the Temple*, the *Assumption*, and the *Nativity of the Virgin*. At the third altar on the left is a late work by Titian, the *Pentecost*. The marble sculpture on the main altar represents the *Plague fleeing before the Virgin* and is by Giusto Le Court. The large sacristy contains a wealth of unforgettable Titian masterpieces: the *Death of Abel*, the *Sacrifice of Abraham*, and *David and Goliath*, dated 1543 on the ceiling, and over the altar, a youthful work of 1512, *St. Mark and other saints*. The works of other artists adorn the walls. Outstanding among these is one of Tintoretto's most famous paintings, the *Wedding at Cana.*

SAN ZACCARIA

This is one of the most interesting churches in Venice. Built in the 9th century, it was altered in the 15th and 16th centuries by Antonio Gambello and Mauro Coducci. Coducci also designed the distinctive six-section façade one of the foremost architectural designs to have come out of the Venetian Renaissance. The statue of *St. Zacharias* above the portal is by Alessandro Vittoria.

THE INTERIOR - Lofty columns divide the side aisles from the nave of this church which has a Gothic apse and peribolus with radiating chapels. The walls are hung with impressive paintings by the major late 17th century Venetian masters. At the second altar on the left is a famous altarpiece by Giovanni Bellini, the *Virgin and Child with saints*, painted in 1505. From the right aisle we enter the *Cappella di Sant'Anastasio* which contains exquisite carved Gothic choir stalls (1455-1464), a *Virgin and Child* by Palma the Elder and, over the entrance, the *Birth of St. John the Baptist* by Tintoretto. From here we enter another chapel with a polygonal apse, the *Cappella di San Tarsio*. A real gem, the chapel contains important ceiling frescoes representing *God the Father and saints* painted in 1442 by the celebrated Florentine master Andrea del Castagno and, on the walls, three magnificent altarpieces by Giovanni d'Alemagna and Antonio Vivarini. At the end of the left aisle is the tomb, with self-portrait, of the sculptor Alessandro Vittoria buried here in 1605. Vittoria also left two exquisite holy water fonts in this church.

CAMPO SANTI GIOVANNI E PAOLO

After Piazza San Marco this is the most impressive of the Venetian campi. Looking onto the square are the façades of the church of Santi Giovanni e Paolo and the Scuola Grande di San Marco, with the adjoining church of San Lazzaro dei Mendicanti. In the middle is the *Equestrian Monument to Bartolomeo Colleoni,* condottiere (captain) of the Republic. This masterpiece of Renaissance art was begun by the Florentine artist Andrea del Verrocchio (1488) and finished by Alessandro Leopardi in 1496.

SANTI GIOVANNI E PAOLO

Started by the Dominican friars in 1246, it was not finished until 1430. Like its Franciscan counterpart, Santa Maria Gloriosa dei Frari, it is an outstanding example of the architectural style known as Venetian Gothic. Inside are the mortal remains of some of the *Serenissima's* best-known figures. The façade contains Byzantine sculpture and combines Gothic with Renaissance elements (carved portal by Bartolomeo Bon) but was never finished.

THE INTERIOR - It is in the form of a Latin cross with three aisles and a cluster of five apses. Around the doorway are three tombs of members of the Mocenigo family, the finest of which was built for Doge Pietro Mocenigo by Pietro Lombardo in 1485 (on the right). Starting at the first altar of the right aisle is a *Virgin and Saints* by Francesco Bissolo and at the second the *San Vincenzo Ferreri Altarpiece* by Giovanni Bellini (1465). After the Addolorata Chapel, which leads to the Baptistry, we come to the monument to the Valier family doges by Andrea Tirali (18th century). At the end of the aisle is an elaborately decorated chapel, the Cappella di San

The Church of San Zanipolo (Santi Giovanni e Paolo).

Domenico, whose ceiling fresco representing *St. Dominic in Glory* is one of the masterpieces of Piazzetta (1727). In the right transept, *Jesus carrying the Cross* by Alvise Vivarini, *St. Anthony and the poor* by Lorenzo Lotto (1542) and, by the second altar, *Christ and saints* by Rocco Marconi. The 15th century Gothic window by Bartolomeo Vivarini is truly magnificent. The choir: it conveys a majestic effect with its lightfilled polygonal apse and Baroque main altar. On the right is the 14th century monument to Doge Michele Morosini, with a mosaic *Crucifixion* and, a bit further on, the monument to Doge Leonardo Loredan of 1572. To the left are monuments

The Church of San Zanipolo: the interior.

to two other doges, Doge Andrea Vendramin by Pietro and Tullio Lombardo (15th century) and Doge Marco Corner with a statue of the *Virgin* by Nino Pisano. At the far side of the left transept is a monument to Doge Antonio Venier by the Dalle Masegnes and below it is the entrance to the 16th century Chapel of the Rosary, once adorned with sculpture by Alessandro Vittoria and paintings by Tintoretto, Bassano, and others (unfortunately burnt in a fire in 1867). The reconstructed ceiling contains three works by Veronese: the *Annunciation*, the *Assumption*, and the *Adoration of the Shepherds*. Along the walls are 18th century sclptures and a pair of bronze candlesticks by Alessandro Vittoria. From the left aisle we enter the elegant Sacristy adorned with paintings by Palma the Younger. Further on, funerary monuments to Doge Pasquale Malipiero by Pietro Lombardo, Senator Bonzi, Doge Tommaso Mocenigo by 15th century Florentine artists, and, lastly, Nicolò Marcello by Pietro Lombardo. A statue of *St. Jerome* by Alessandro Vittoria adorns the first left aisle altar.

MADONNA DELL'ORTO

According to an old tradition, a miraculous statue of the Virgin (today preserved inside the Church) was found in the *orto* (garden) which originally covered this area. The façade is an attractive mixture of the Romanesque and Gothic styles. The statues of the

Apostles in the upper niches of the sides of the façade are by followers of the Dalle Masegnes.

THE INTERIOR - Of basilican plan, it has three aisles divided by marble columns and a polygonal apse. The church contains numerous paintings by Jacopo Robusti, better known as Tintoretto, who was buried here in 1594. His tomb, marked by a simple stone plaque, is inside the church to the right of the choir. By the first altar of the right aisle is *St. John in Ecstasy with other saints*, the masterpiece of Cima da Conegliano (1493). Above the Cappella di San Mauro is Tintoretto's *Presentation of the Virgin at the Temple*. The paintings in the choir (the *Last Judgment, Adoration of the Golden Calf*, and *Moses receiving the Tablets of the Law*) are all by Titian who painted them when he had reached the height of his creative powers. In the fourth chapel off the left aisle is another Tintoretto, *St. Agnes raising Licinus from the dead*. The *Virgin and Child* in the first chapel is by Giovanni Bellini.

SANTI APOSTOLI

This church's origins go way back, although it was remodelled several times until 1575 when it was radically restructured to its present from. On the Campo di Santi Apostoli note a house oddly nestled in between the belltower and the dome of the Corner Chapel. The belltower of 1672 was completed by a bellchamber designed by Andrea Tirali.

THE INTERIOR - Inside the rectangular single-aisled church, we first note the ceiling with frescoes of the *Glorification of the Eucharist* and the *Apostles* by Fabio Canal and G. Gaspari (1748). The Cappella Corner on the right side was remodelled in the 16th century; its Lombardo-style architecture has been attributed to Mauro Coducci. On the right wall is the tomb of Marco Corner attributed to Tullio Lombardo, the one on the left is the tomb of Cardinal Giorgio Corner. On the altar is a fine altarpiece depicting the *Communion of St. Lucy* by Giovan Battista Tiepolo and, on the altar of the next chapel, a painting of the *Nativity of the Virgin* by Giorgio Contarini. In another of the righthand chapels we can see the remains of Byzantine frescoes showing the *Deposition from the Cross* and the *Burial of Christ*. Nearby is a relief depicting *St. Sebastian*, a 16th century work by Tullio Lombardo. In the choir, on the right, is a *Last Supper* by Cesare da Conegliano (16th century) and, on the left, the *Shower of Manna* by followers of Paolo Veronese.

CARMINI

Sebastiano Mariani added a Renaissance façade to this 14th century church at the beginning of the 15th century. A portal preeceded by a porch has been preserved from the original building on the left side.

THE INTERIOR · The two aisles are divided from the nave by fine 14th century columns with beautifully carved capitals. The extensive fresco cycle on *Episodes from the History of the Carmelite Order* was executed by various artists between the second half of the 17th and first half of the 18th centuries. Among the art treasures contained in the church are the altarpiece with the *Adoration of the shepherds, Sts. Helen, Catherine, and Tobias and the Angel* by Cima da Conegliano (second bay of the right aisle), a relief with the *Deposition* by Francesco di Giorgio Martini (in the sacristy) and *St. Nicholas and other saints* by Lorenzo Lotto (second bay in the left aisle).

The Church of San Barnaba.

SAN BARNABA

The church was built between 1749 and 1776 by Lorenzo Boschetti. The simple façade, resembles a classical temple front with tall columns surmounted by a tympanum. The handsome 14th century brick belltower sports a cone-shaped cusp.

THE INTERIOR - The aisleless interior is adorned with Corinthian columns set into the nave walls. The ceiling was frescoed by a follower of Tiepolo's, Costantino Cedini, and shows *St. Barnabas in Glory*. The *Birth of the Virgin* by Foler is at the first altar on the right. The most interesting works, however, are in the choir: *St. Barnabas and other saints* by Damiano Mazzo on the main altar, the *Climb to Calvary* and the *Last Supper* by Palma the Younger on the walls, and, above the altar, a painting of the *Holy Family* by Paolo Veronese.

SAN FRANCESCO DELLA VIGNA

The building itself was designed by Jacopo Sansovino in the 16th century, while the beautifully-proportioned façade, with its imposing portal flanked by four columns and crowned by a tympanum (gable), is an outstanding neo-Classical design by Palladio.

THE INTERIOR - The interior is in the form of a Latin cross with a single nave. Some noteworthy works of art are to be found inside the church. By the first altar in the transept is a rare painting by the 15th century painter, Antonio da Negroponte. This *Virgin enthroned in adoration* reveals the artist's lively imagination and delicate, harmonious style. In the chapel to the left of the choir are several fine sculptures by Pietro Lombardo and his followers. From the left transept we enter the Cappella Santa which contains a *Virgin and Saints* by Giovanni Bellini (1507). A triptych with *Sts. Jerome, Bernard, and Louis*, by Antonio Vivarini is in the sacristy and a *Sacra Conversazione* painted by Veronese in 1551 is in the fifth chapel on the left.

I GESUATI

Known also as Santa Maria del Rosario, the church was erected between 1726 and 1743 for the Dominican friars who commissioned the architect Giorgio Massari to design a church to replace a 14th century monastery called the «Monastery of the Poor Jesuates». The façade is a handsome interpretation of the Classical style.

THE INTERIOR - The elliptical-shaped church is aisleless with a domed choir and side chapels. The ceiling frescoes by G. B. Tiepolo represent *St. Dominic in Glory*, the *Institution of the Rosary, St. Dominic and the Virgin*, and the *Mysteries of the Rosary*. Starting our tour of the altars from the right side, first altar, the *Virgin in Glory with three saints*, a masterpiece painted by Tiepolo in 1747; second altar, *St. Dominic* by G. B. Piazzetta (1739). The dome frescoes in the choir are by Tiepolo. The main altar and choir stalls are fine 18th century works. The *Virgin and St. Anne* was painted by M. Ignoli. On the left side (third altar) is a dramatic *Crucifixion* by Tintoretto. On the first left altar: Sts. Pius Vth, Thomas Aquinas and Peter the Martyr by Sebastiano Ricci.

CHURCH OF THE JESUITS

Although this grandiose church was established in the 12th century for the Order of the Cross-bearers it was turned over to the Jesuits in 1656 and remodelled by Domenico Rossi between 1715 and 1730. The imposing Baroque façade designed by Fattoretto is adorned with statues of the 12 *Apostles* (by F. Penso, the Groppelli brothers, and P. Baratta). There is also a fine portal with *Angels* by Matteo Calderoni.

THE INTERIOR - The single-aisled church has a Latin-cross plan and is wholly decorated with striking patterns of colored marble inlay. The stucco ceiling is by A. Stazio and the frescoes by Fontebasso. On the wall by the entrance is a monument by G. B. Longhena and a bust of *Priamo Da Lezze* by Jacopo Sansovino. On the first altar on the right, the *Guardian Angel* by Palma the Younger, in the second, a statue of *St. Barbara* by Morlaiter, and in the third, *Virgin and saints* by Balestra. In the right transept is a statue of *St. Ignatius* by P. Baratta. In the chapel to the right of the main chapel is *St. Francis Xavier preaching* by P. Liberi. The choir has elaborate architecture influenced by the style of Bernini by Father G. Pozzo, sculptures by Torretto, and frescoes by L. Dorigny. Two outstanding paintings are hanging here: the *Assumption of the Virgin* by Jacopo Tintoretto and the *Martyrdom of St. Laurence* by Titian.

SAN GIOVANNI IN BRAGORA

Although its origins date back to the 8th century, the church was completely rebuilt in 1475. The strange name «*Bragora*» could either be derived from *agorà*, ancient Greek for square, or «*bràgola*» (marketplace) in Venetian dialect. The façade is one of the finest examples of the late Venetian Gothic style.

THE INTERIOR - It has three aisles and a Gothic-style raftered ceiling. Over the entrance, *Christ before Caiaphas* by Palma the Younger. On the nave walls and the triumphal arch, the *Annunciation, saints,* and other 15th century frescoes by a provincial artist, Tommaso di Zorzi. In the second chapel of the right aisle, an altarpiece with *St. John the Almoner,* and, in the lunette, the *Removal of the body of St. John to Venice* by Jacopo Marieschi (the mortal remains of the saint are in an urn beneath the altar). At the end of the right aisle over the sacristy door is a painting of *Christ blessing* by Alvise Vivarini (1493). The Renaissance choir was built by Sebastiano Mariani between 1485 and 1488. On the pillars by the entrance are two works by Vivarini, *St. Helen and Constantine by the Cross* on the right and *Christ Resurrected* on the left. On the main altar are three sculptures: *Faith* by Antonio Gai, *St. John the Evangelist, and St. John the Almoner* by Giovanni Marchiori. In the apse is a fine *Baptism of Christ* by Cima da Conegliano. On the walls the *Last Suppper* by Paris Bordone and the *Washing of the Feet* by Palma the Younger. In the left aisle, in the chapel closest to the choir, are two noteworthy altarpieces: a triptych representing the *Virgin between Sts. Andrew and John the Baptist,* by Bartolomeo Vivarini on the right and *Sts. Andrew, Jerome, and Martin* on the left by Francesco Bissolo.

SAN GIOVANNI CRISOSTOMO

Once this church looked out on the Grand Canal, although after being gutted in a fire in 1475, it was rebuilt between 1497 and 1504 by Mauro Coducci on its present location. The façade with its curvilinear design is extremely elegant. The belltower was built in the 1500s.

THE INTERIOR - The church is in the shape of a Greek cross, with barrel vaults and a dome at the crossing. The first altar on the right is adorned with a late work by Giovanni Bellini, *Sts. Christopher, Jerome, and Augustine*. On either side of the altar are organ panels painted by Giovanni Mansueti. On the main altar is a celebrated altarpiece by Sebastiano del Piombo showing *St. John Chrysostomos and other saints*, painted in the early 1500s.

SAN GIOVANNI ELEMOSINARIO

Originally built in 1071, it was gutted in a fire in 1513 and reconstructed by Scarpagnino in 1530. The belltower, unscathed by the fire, is the original one put up between 1398 and 1410.

THE INTERIOR - In the shape of a Greek cross, it is covered with a dome. On the entrance wall is a *Crucifixion* by L. Corona who also painted the *Shower of Manna* on the right wall. In the chapel to the right of the main one is a fine painting by Pordenone depicting *Sts. Sebastian, Catherine, and Roch*. In the sacristy the ceiling fresco of *St. Augustine* and the *Virgin and St. Philip* on the altar are by G. V. Pittoni. In the choir by the main altar is a masterpiece painted by Titian in 1545, *St. John the Almoner*. In the lunette, the *Resurrection* by L. Corona and, on the walls, two other works by the same artist representing the *Sermon in the Garden* and the *Crucifixion*. The *Last Supper* on the left is by Aliense. On the left wall of the church is *Constantine with the cross* by Palma the Younger and, on the door beside, are three panel paintings by Marco Vercellio. They represent *St. John the Almoner, Doge Donato visiting the church*, and *St. Mark*.

SAN GIORGIO MAGGIORE

The church's stark white façade stands out impressively against the ochre-hued buildings crowding it. One of Palladio's finest designs (the great architect worked on the project between 1565 and 1580), the basilica was finished in 1610 by Scamozzi who kept faithfully to the master's original plans. The façade once more reveals Palladio's distinctive style: the space is divided into three sections by four columns topped by Corinthian capitals. In the two niches between the columns are statues of *Sts. George* and *Stephen* and, on either side busts of *Doges Tribuno Mommo* and *P. Zini* by Giulio Moro. The belltower was put up by the Bolognese

The Church of San Giorgio Maggiore on the Island of San
Giorgio.

architect Benedetto Buratti in 1791 to replace an older one which
collapsed in 1773.

THE INTERIOR - Stark yet imposing, the single-aisled church is in the
shape of an inverted Latin cross. In the second altar on the right is a
wooden *Crucifix* by the great Florentine artist, Michelozzo. On the main
altar of the choir is a superb bronze group by Girolamo Campagna (1593).
Two great Tintorettos are hanging on the walls: the *Last Supper* on the
right and the *Shower of Manna* on the left.

SANTA MARIA FORMOSA

Although the original church of Santa Maria Formosa was
erected much earlier, it was rebuilt by Mauro Coducci in 1492. It
has two 16th century façades and a 17th century Baroque belfry.

THE INTERIOR - In the shape of a Latin cross, it has no side aisles. In the
first chapel on the right is a superb triptych by Bartolomeo Vivarini. The
scenes depicted are the *Nativity of the Virgin*, the *Virgin of Mercy*, and the
Meeting of Joachim and St. Anne. In the right transept is a renowned
altarpiece, *St. Barbara and four saints*, painted by Palma the Elder in 1509.

SANTA MARIA DEI MIRACOLI

Pietro Lombardo designed this Renaissance church in 1481. Its unusual and very attractive façade sports marble decoration on two storeys and a central portal surmounted by two huge windows.

THE INTERIOR - The walls of the rectangular church are lined in precious marbles and the coffered ceiling is divided into 50 lacunars with heads of prophets and saints by Pier Maria Pennacchi (1528). The raised choir, a masterpiece of decorative art created by the Lombardo brothers, is reached by an elegant staircase. The main altar is surmounted by a dome.

SAN MOISE'

There has been a church on this spot since the 8th century A.D. In the 10th century the original structure was rebuilt by a certain Moisè Venier who dedicated it to his own name-saint, St. Moisè. Later, in the 14th century, the lovely belltower with its distinctive brick spire was raised alongside it. The Baroque façade was designed in the second half of the 17th century by Alessandro Tremignon for Vincenzo Fini whose bust can be seen on the obelisk above the central portal (although Tremignon commissioned the sculptor Enrico Meyiring with the actual execution of the decorative scheme). Many of the sculptures had to be removed during the 19th century, since they were in danger of crumbling, which means that the decoration which today appears exaggeratedly ornate, was even more so in the original version.

THE INTERIOR - The ceiling of the aisleless church is frescoed with the *Vision of Moses* by Niccolò Bambini. The first altar on the right is adorned with an 18th century marble *Pietà* by Antonio Corradini and a painting in the Caraccis' style representing the *Adoration of the Magi* by Giuseppe Diamantini. Also on the right is a fine pulpit carved in the 18th century by Tagliapietra. In the second altar is the *Finding of the cross* by Pietro Liberi. In the sacristy is a bronze altar frontal with a *Deposition scene* by the 17th century Genoese artists, Niccolò and Sebastiano Roccatagliata. The main altar of the church is an elaborate Baroque creation by Tremignon decorated with sculptures by Meyring. In the choir are 16th century carved wooden choir stalls. The left chapel contains two especially noteworthy works, the *Last Supper* by Palma the Younger and the *Washing of the Feet*, a late work by Jacopo Tintoretto.

SAN POLO

According to tradition the church was founded in 837 by Doge Pietro Gradonico. It was then rebuilt in the Gothic style and remodelled many times. Its lovely belltower dates from 1362.

The Church of San Moisé.

THE INTERIOR · It is in the form of a basilica with three aisles. On the inside façade are two fine works, the *Communion of the Apostles* by Jacopo Tintoretto and the *Baptism of Constantine* by Piazza. Over the first altar on the right is the *Assumption of the Virgin* by Jacopo Tintoretto. In the Cappella del Santissimo Sacramento built in the Lombard style are four paintings by Giuseppe Salviati recounting *Episodes from the Life of Christ*. In the choir are paintings by Palma the Younger: the *Temptation and Liberation of St. Anthony*, and *Conversion of St. Paul*, the *Giving of the Keys to St. Peter*, and *St. Mark Preaching*. In addition, there are two paintings by G. B. Tiepolo representing *Angels in Glory* and the *Via Crucis*. On the main altar, between bronze statues of *St. Paul* and *St. Anthony Abbot* by Vittoria, is a 15th century painted *Crucifix*. The chapel to the left of the high altar contains a *Vistation* by Veronese. At the second altar on the left is the *Virgin with St. John Nepomucenus* by G. B. Tiepolo.

IL REDENTORE

The church is the result of Andrea Palladio's architectural genius combined with the technical skill of Antonio Da Ponte who built it between 1577 and 1592. It was put up in thanksgiving for the cessation of another of the innumerable plague epidemics which had taken its toll of Venetian victims. A huge staircase leads up to façade proper which consists of a single order of columns surmounted by a tympanum. Crowning the church is a dome flanked by a pair of belltowers.

THE INTERIOR - The inside reflects the classical harmony of the outside. The stately colonnade along the aisleless interior confers a majestic effect to the whole. The Baroque main altar is adorned with bronzes by Campagna. It the sacristy are some interesting works, including a *Virgin and Child* by Alvise Vivarini, a *Baptism of Christ* by a follower of Veronese, a *Virgin and Child with Saints* by Palma the Younger, and several works by Bassano.

SAN SALVADOR

Although this is one of the oldest churches in Venice, it has been remodelled over the centuries, first in the 16th century by Giorgio Spavento, then by Tullio Lombardo, and lastly by Sansovino and Scamozzi, who gave it its present appearance. The intricate carved Baroque façade is by Bernardino Falcone (1663).

THE INTERIOR - Not only one of the finest examples of Venetian Renaissance architecture extant, this three-aisled church is also filled with masterpieces of art. Between the second and third altars of the right aisle is the tomb monument to Doge Francesco Venier with statues of *Charity* and *Hope* by Sansovino. A grandiose painting of the *Annunciation* by Titian (1566) adorns the third altar. The main altar contains an embossed silver altar frontal, a superb example of Venetian 14th century craftsmanship. It is surmounted by a *Transfiguration* by Titian. In the chapel to the left of the main chapel is the *Supper at Emmaus*, recently attributed to Giovanni Bellini.

SAN SEBASTIANO

The church was built in the 1500s by Francesco da Castiglione, assisted by Scarpagnino. It was restored in 1867. Inside is the finest collection of Veronese's paintings to be found anywhere in Venice. (Veronese himself was buried in the church in 1588).

THE INTERIOR - The decoration of this single-aisle church was commissioned from Paolo Veronese whose exuberant youth and vigor are plainly visible. Unfortunately, Veronese was confined to a wall space that hardly lent itself to fresco painting, so he had to overcome difficult technical problems relating to poor lighting and tight spaces. The most noteworthy paintings are the *Story of Esther* in the ceiling panels, the *Virgin with St. Sebastian and other saints* by the altar of the main chapel, the *Martyrdom* by *Sts. Mark and Marcellinus* on the left, the *Martyrdom of St. Sebastian* on the right, and the *Annunciation* on the triumphal arch. In the chapel to the left of the main chapel are a bust of Veronese and, on the ground, his tomb slab, as well as an organ with panels decorated by the great master. The sacristy contains paintings by various followers of Veronese and, on the ceiling, five panels which were the first works the great artist from Verona painted in Venice.

SANTO STEFANO

This late 13th century Romanesque-Gothic church has been restored many times over the centuries. The façade has distinctive single and double mullioned windows and a fine International Gothic Style portal executed by the Bon brothers.

THE INTERIOR - The striking interior has three aisles divided by columns of Greek marble and red marble from Verona and a keel-shaped wooden beamed ceiling. A number of art treasures are to be found here. In the sacristy are three Tintorettos: the *Last Supper*, the *Washing of the Feet*, and *Christ in the garden of Gethsemane*. The altarpiece depicting *Sts. Peter and Laurence* is by Bartolomeo Vivarini, the *Archangel Raphael* and *saints* by Piazzetta and the *Virgin with saints* by Palma the Elder. In the choir with its huge polygonal apse are magnificent 15th century Gothic choir stalls. From the left aisle we enter the splendid 16th century *cloister*, attributed to Scarpagnino, which was once adorned with frescoes by Pordenone.

SAN TROVASO

«Trovaso» is a Venetian contracted version of Gervase and Protasius, two important saints. Already in existence by the 11th cent., the church was burnt to the ground and rebuilt 1583.

THE INTERIOR - The interior has a huge choir and side chapels. At the third altar on the right is *St. Francis of Paola, Faith, and Charity* by Alvise di Friso. On the wall nearby is a *Virgin and Child* by a follower of Giovanni Bellini. In the right transept is a lovely altar frontal, a Renaissance relief attributed to Pietro Lombardo, which portrays *Angels with the symbols of the Passion*. In the chapel to the right of the main chapel is a *Crucifixion* by Domenico Tintoretto on the altar. A Gothic masterpiece, *St. Chrysogonus on horseback* adorns the walls. It has been attributed by some to Jacobello del Fiore and by others to Michele Giambono. The choir contains the *Adoration of the Magi* and *Joachim expelled from the Temple* by Jacopo Tintoretto and his pupils. In the chapel to the left of the main chapel is a *Temptation of St. Anthony* by Jacopo Tintoretto. The sacristy contains a *Virgin* by Rosalba Carriera and *Sts. John and Mary Magdalene* attributed to Tintoretto. In the Chapel of the Holy Sacrament in the left transept are other paintings by Tintoretto.

THE SURROUNDINGS OF VENICE

We shall now turn to the group of splendid islands which are like gemstones laid out amidst the lagoon, the most precious of which is Venice herself. There are all kinds, ranging in size from tiny uninhabited islets to good-sized islands, now sleepy fishing villages, but once thriving cities. An excursion to Torcello, Burano, Murano is a must for those who would like to really know Venice. These island towns are fascinating not only for the art treasures they possess, but also for their hauntingly beautiful landscapes in an atmosphere of magical silence - and this is not all the lagoon has to offer. We must not forget the local crafts; glassblowing, lacemaking, and coppercrafting are some of the typical ones practiced by the local artisans.

Lido of Venice.

THE LIDO OF VENICE

The Lido is actually an elongated island about a mile from Venice, bordered by a considerable stretch of sandy beach. Once the city's natural defense, it is now a celebrated resort. The Lido's international reputation comes from its superbly equipped hotels and excellent tourist accommodations, its fine beach, and the cultural, artistic, and sports events held here throughout the year.

From the smart worldliness of the Lido with its elegant hotels and bathing establishments, we pass to the enchanting peacefulness of the mysterious **Isle of San Lazzaro degli Armeni**. Here, a community of Armenian monks has been thriving for centuries, immersed in the silence of their convent, surrounded by luxuriant vegetation. The atmosphere of the island is permeated with memories of Byron who spent lengthy periods of his life on San Lazzaro. Sailing towards Murano we encounter the **Island of San Michele in Isola** where, according to legend, St. Romualdo, founder of the Camaldolese Order once lived (although the order held on to the island until the 19th century, today it is just a sleepy cemetery marked by majestic cypresses). Proceeding toward Burano and Torcello we encounter, on the left, the solitary **Islet of San Giacomo in Palude** and, on the right, the lovely **Islet of San Francesco del Deserto**, where solitude and silence reign over the thick vegetation surrounding the hermitage. We shall now take a closer look at the major lagoon centers, Murano with its glass factories, Burano with its lacemakers, and the former rival of Venice, Torcello.

MURANO

Murano: Church of Santi Maria e Donato.

Less than a mile away from Venice, Murano is a typical lagoon town spread over five islets. It is renowned for its glassblowing industry which dates back to the 13th century. The **Glass Museum** in the **Palazzo Giustiniani** exhibits rare pieces of the glassblower's art, including Roman and Egyptian objects dating from Antiquity to the 18th century.

Side view of the Church of Santi Maria e Donato; products of Venetian glass blowers in the foreground.

Santi Maria e Donato – The church originally on the site was rebuilt in the 12th century. It is a unique example of the Venetian Byzantine style with its unusual hexagonal apse and double tier of columns creating a graceful pattern of niches and loggias.

THE INTERIOR - The church has a basilican plan and three aisles divided from each other by ten marble columns with superb Corinthian capitals. The marble flooring dates from the 12th century. At the beginning of the left wall is a painted carved altarpiece of large dimensions which is an outstanding example of 14th century Venetian art.

San Pietro Martire – Inside this 14th century church are numerous works of art. Three of the finest are Giovanni Bellini's *Virgin enthroned with two angels and saints* and *Assumption of the Virgin and saints*, and Veronese's *St. Jerome in the Desert* over the sacristy door.

BURANO

Burano (originally Burianum or Boreanum) occupies four tiny islands inhabited mainly by fisherman. It was first settled in the 5th-6th centuries by refugees from Altinum fleeing Attila's terrible Huns. Though it is mostly famous for the traditional art of lacemaking which the women of the town have been handing down to their daughters for centuries, Burano also boasts remarkable artistic treasures.

117

Burano: the famous laces.

Taking the main road of the village named after its best-known native son, the 18th century composer Baldassarre Galuppi, known as «*Il Buranello*», we soon reach the main square and the 16th century **church of San Martino**. Alongside is its eighteenth century belltower which, like the Tower of Pisa, leans dangerously to one side, and the **chapel of Santa Barbara** which contains works of great interest, such as Tiepolo's huge *Crucifixion* (dated c. 1725), *St. Mark and other saints* by Girolamo da Santacroce, and several canvases by Giovanni Mansueti (end of the 16th century). On the same square stands the **Palazzo della Podestà**, a 19th century building now occupied by the **Lacemaking School**, which was founded in 1872 so that the secrets of this ancient art would never be lost.

TORCELLO

Only six miles from Venice is one of the most fascinating spots in the lagoon. Now just a solitary village on a lonely island, it was once a flourishing hub of culture and commerce whose greatness dimmed as Venice's grew. All that is left of its ancient splendour is a group of monuments surrounding a picturesque grassy square where the so-called «*caregon*», which, if popular tradition is to be believed, was originally Attila's throne, stands.

The Cathedral – Consecrated to St. Maria Assunta, the Cathedral's origins go back to the year 639, although it was rebuilt in

Torcello: the Church of Santa Fosca.

the early 11th century together with its majestic belltower. Ruins of a circular-plan 8th century baptistry are visible in front of the building.

THE INTERIOR · Austere and simple, the church has three aisles divided from each other by columns. The inner façade is entirely covered with remarkable 12th-13th century Byzantine mosaics portraying the *Last Judgement*. In the nave are two pulpits and an iconostasis (rood screen) with exquisite transennae supporting a series of 15th century icons. In the triumphal arch is a 12th century mosaic representing the *12 Apostles* and, in the semi-dome, one of the *Virgin and Child* dating from the 13th century.

Santa Fosca – The church, built around the 11th century, has an unusual octagonal shape. On the outside a portico resting on arches runs around five sides of the building, while the simple Greek cross interior has columns with Byzantine capitals.

On the square are two Gothic buildings, the **Palazzo del Consiglio** and the **Palazzo dell'Archivio**. They contain a fascinating collection of archeological finds discovered on the lagoon islands, but mainly on Torcello.

USEFUL INFORMATION

The last pages of the guide contain practical information on Museums, Hotels, Public and Private Transport facilities and other useful hints for a visitor in Venice. Various sign-post along the main tourist itineraries make it easier to get to the more important Museums and Monuments.

MAIN PUBLIC NAVIGATIONAL FACILITIES

Public transport in Venice relies on water-buses, water-taxis and ferryboats. Water-buses, which stop at each landing stage, offer a veritable excursion through the heart of Venice.
Timetables of each water-bus (vaporetto) line are affixed at each landing stage.
Line No. 1 - The slow (accelerato) version - is the most worthwhile choice for the visitor: it stops at a great number of wharfs all along the Grand Canal on its way from Piazzale Roma to Venice-Lido, as one can see on the diagram below right.

Trough Lines

P.le Roma - Stazione - Rialto - S. Marco - Lido
Slow (accelerato) and Direct Lines
P.le Roma, Tronchetto - S. Marco

Circular Lines

Fondamenta Nuove - S. Michele - Murano - Fondamenta Nuove - Arsenale - S. Zaccaria - Isola di S. Giorgio Maggiore - Giudecca - P.le Roma - Stazione - Cannaregio

External Lines

Venezia, Zattere - Giudecca
Venezia, S. Zaccaria - Lido
Venezia, Fondamenta Nuove - Murano - Burano - Torcello
Venezia, Fondamenta Nuove - Murano - S. Erasmo
Venezia, S. Zaccaria - Lido - Punta Sabbioni
Venezia, Tronchetto - Lido - Punta Sabbioni (Ferry-Boat)

Venezia, S. Zaccaria - S. Servolo - S. Lazzaro degli Armeni
Venezia, S. Zaccaria - S. Maria delle Grazie - S. Clemente
Venezia, Zattere - Fusina
Venezia, Fondamenta Nuove - Mestre, S. Giuliano

1. Piazzale Roma
2. Ferrovia
3. Riva Biasio
4. S. Marcuola
5. S. Stae
6. Ca' d'Oro
7. Rialto
8. S. Silvestro
9. S. Angelo
10. S. Tomà
11. Ca' Rezzonico
12. Accademia
13. S. Maria d. Giglio
14. Salute
15. S. Marco
16. S. Zaccaria
17. Arsenale
18. Giardini
19. S. Elena
20. Lido di Venezia

MUSEUMS - GALLERIES - EXHIBITIONS

Archeological Museum, S. Marco - ☎ 25978
Oriental Museum, Cà Pesaro - ☎ 27681
Correr Museum, S. Marco - ☎ 25625
18th Century Venice Museum, Cà Rezzonico - ☎ 24543
Glass Museum, Murano, Fondamenta Giustinian - ☎ 739586
Fortuny Museum, San Beneto - ☎ 700995
Natural History Museum, Fondaco dei Turchi - ☎ 35885
Sacred Bizantin Icon Museum, Ponte dei Greci - ☎ 26581
Naval Historical Museum, Arsenale - ☎ 700276
Jewish Community Museum, Ghetto Nuovo - ☎ 715012
Estuary Museum, Torcello - ☎ 730761
Lace Museum, Burano - ☎ 730034
Diocese Museum of Liturgical Art, Chiostro di S. Apollonia, S. Marco - ☎ 29166
Academy Galleries, Accademia - ☎ 22247
Gallery of Modern Art, Cà Pesaro - ☎ 24127
Museum of St. Mark's - ☎ 25205
Golden Altar Screen and Treasure Vault, Basilica di S. Marco, ☎ 25697
Goldoni House, S. Tomà - ☎ 36353
Querini-Stampalia Picture Gallery, S.M. Formosa - ☎ 25235
Manfrediniana Picture Gallery, Seminario Patriarcale, Campo della Salute - ☎ 25558
Guggenheim Collection, S. Gregorio - ☎ 29347
Torcello Cathedral - ☎ 730084
Island of San Lazzaro degli Armeni - ☎ 760104
Island of San Francesco del Deserto - ☎ 86863
Great School of San Rocco, S. Rocco - ☎ 34864
Great School of San Giorgio degli Schiavoni, S. Antonin - ☎ 28828
Great School of the Carmel, Carmini - ☎ 26553
School of St. John the Evangelist, Campo S. Giovanni Evangelista - ☎ 24134
International Contemporary Art Biennal Exhibition, Giardini di Castello - ☎ 700311/20578
Aquarium, S. Zaccaria - ☎ 707770

LIBRARIES

Library of St. Mark's, S. Marco
Correr Library, S. Marco
Querini Stampalia Library, S.M. Formosa
Library of the Giorgio Cini Foundation, Island of S. Giorgio Maggiore
Library of the Historical Archives of the International Contemporary Art Biennal Exhibition, S. Croce
Civil Library of Mestre, via Piave

EMERGENCY TELEPHONE NUMBERS

Police - Public Rescue - ☎ 113
Marco Polo Airport - ☎ 661111
Airport Information Office - ☎ 661262
Airport Lost Property Office - ☎ 661266
Port Authority - S. Marco - ☎ 705600 - Zattere - ☎ 703044
Carabinieri Emergency Station - Venezia-Mestre - ☎ 112
Carabinieri - Piazzale Roma - ☎ 5235333
Railway Information Bureau - ☎ 715555
Town Hall - ☎ 788111
Police (Emergency Squad) - Venezia - ☎ 113
Police - S. Chiara - ☎ 5222331
Police (Emergency Squad) - Mestre - ☎ 57777
Highway Police - Mestre - ☎ 961722/56111
First Aid Post - Venezia - ☎ 5230000
First Aid Post - Mestre - ☎ 988988
Police Headquarters and Passport Office ☎ 703222
Customs - Mestre - ☎ 984877/984971
Customs - Aeroporto Tessera - ☎ 950530/964390
Automobile Club Rescue Station - ☎ 116
Fire Brigade - Venezia - ☎ 5222222/5222223
Fire Brigade - Mestre - ☎ 972222
Fire Brigade - Lido - ☎ 5260222
City Police - Venezia - ☎ 5224063
City Police - Piazzale Roma - ☎ 5222612/5224576
City Police - Tronchetto - ☎ 5286973
City Police - Mestre - ☎ 5056103
City Police - Lido - ☎ 5260395
Town Hall Tourist Office - ☎ 5200792
Railway Lost Poperty Office - ☎ 716122/5289600
Permanent Medical Post - Lido - ☎ 768700

CASINOS

Venice - ☎ 710211
Lido - ☎ 767054

TOURIST INFORMATION

Visitors and Tourism Company (A.A.S.T.) - Palazzo Martinengo Rialto 4089 - ☎ 5226110/5230313
Provincial Tourism Organisation (E.P.T.) - S. Marco Ascensione 71c - ☎ 5226356
Tourist Guide Association - ☎ 709038
Youth Hostel Venezia - ☎ 38211

WATER TAXIS

Cooperativa S. Marco - ☎ 22303
Serenissima - ☎ 28538/24281
Cooperativa Fondamenta Nuove - ☎ 37313

Cooperativa Veneziana - ☎ 716922
Cooperativa Libertà - ☎ 28206/706190
Motoscafi S. Lucia - ☎ 718235

GONDOLAS

Bacino Orseolo - ☎ 89316
Calle Vallaresso - ☎ 706120
Danieli - ☎ 22254
Ferrovia - ☎ 23543
Piazzale Roma - ☎ 20581
Isola Tronchetto - ☎ 38919
S. Maria del Giglio - ☎ 22073
S. Sofia - ☎ 22844
Trinità (S. Moisé) - ☎ 31837/23103

TAXIS (CABS)

Piazzale Roma - ☎ 37774
Lido - S. Maria Elisabetta - ☎ 765974/765975
Lido - Casinò Municipale - ☎ 761064
Mestre - Stazione - ☎ 929499
Mestre - Piazza Ferretto - ☎ 57942
Mestre - Via Piave - ☎ 936222

PORTERS

Ferrovia S. Lucia - ☎ 715272
Accademia - ☎ 24891
S. Zaccaria - ☎ 28901
S.M. Formosa - ☎ 35615
Bacino Orseolo - ☎ 700545
Rialto - ☎ 705308
Bragora - ☎ 87273
Vallaresso - ☎ 24412
S. Geremia - ☎ 715694
S. Marco - ☎ 32385
S. Moisè - ☎ 37578
Piazzale Roma - ☎ 23590/703070
S. Simeon - ☎ 703801
Stazione F.S. Mestre - ☎ 929483

CONSULATES

Argentine - Cannaregio, SS. Apostoli, 4392 - ☎ 27503
Belgium - Cannaregio, S. Giovanni Crisostomo, 5768 - ☎ 24124
Bolivia - S. Marco, Calle del Cappello Nero, 163 - ☎ 86718
Brasil - Mestre, Via Fapanni, 32 - ☎ 57218
Columbia - Dorsoduro, Salute, 131 - ☎ 703373
Denmark - S. Polo, Sant'Agostin, 2347 - ☎ 706822
Finland - Mestre, S. Giuliano, 4 - ☎ 59912

France - Dorsoduro, Zattere, 1397 - ☎ 22392/24319
Great Britain - Dorsoduro, Accademia, 1051 - ☎ 27207
Greece - S. Polo, Riva del Vin, 720 - ☎ 37260
Holland (Netherlands) - Castello, Riva degli Schiavoni, 4150 - ☎ 38112
Ivory Coast - Mestre, Via Poerio, 34 - ☎ 971200
Lebanon - Dorsoduro, Zattere, 62 - ☎ 25076
Liberia - S. Marco, S. Maria del Giglio, 2472 - ☎ 24809
Luxembourg - Castello, Ponte dell'Angelo, 5312 - ☎ 22047
Mexico - S. Marco, S. Zulian, 235 - ☎ 37445
Monaco (Principality of) - Dorsoduro, Fondamenta Bragadin, 583 - ☎ 29751
Norway - Mestre, Rotonda Garibaldi, 12/7 - ☎ 962050
Panama - Lido, via L. Mocenigo, 21 - ☎ 765233
Perù - Lido, Riviera Santa Maria Elisabetta, 7 - ☎ 764141
Portugal - S. Marco, Ascensione, 1253 - ☎ 23446
Spain - S. Marco, Fondamenta Ostreghe, 2442/A - ☎ 87877
Sweden (c/o Ligabue S.p.A.) - P.le Roma, 499 - ☎ 706888
Switzerland - Dorsoduro, Zattere, 810 - ☎ 703944-25996
United States - Trieste, via Roma, 9 - ☎ 040/68728
Western Germany - S. Marco, San Vidal, 2888 - ☎ 25100

NON-CATHOLIC RELIGIONS

Jewish Temple (Ghetto vecchio) ☎ 715012. Saturday 9.30 A.M.
Evangelical Lutheran Church C.po SS. Apostoli 4443.
Evangelical Valdese and Methodist Church (S. Maria Formosa 5170). ☎ 5227549. Sunday Service 11 A.M.
Greek Orthodox Church (Ponte dei Greci 3412). ☎ 5225446. 11-12 A.M. Sundays and Saints Holidays.
Anglican Church St. George's, Dorsoduro (Campo San Vio, 870) ☎ 5200571. Services 8.30 A.M. and 11.30 A.M. Sermons 10.30 A.M.

BANKS

8.30-13.30 - 15-16. Closed on Saturdays and Sundays.

American Service Bank - S. Marco 1336 - ☎ 705344
Banca Cattolica del Veneto - S. Marco 4481 - ☎ 957066

Banca Commerciale Italiana - Via XXII Marzo 2188 - ☎ 710333

Banca d'America e d'Italia - Via XXII Marzo 2216/17 - ☎ 5200766

Banca d'Italia - S. Marco 4799 - ☎ 708644

Banca Nazionale del Lavoro - Bac. Orseolo 1118/1121 - ☎ 667511

Banca Nazionale delle Comunicazioni - Rio Terrà S. Leonardo 1353 - ☎ 5226722/5234610

Banca Popolare di Novara - S. Marco 4187 S. Luca - ☎ 5231640/5287991

Nuovo Banco Ambrosiano - Via XXII Marzo 2378/a - ☎ 5285413

Banco di Napoli - Campo S. Gallo 1112 - Bacino Orseolo - ☎ 5231700

Banco di Roma - Mercerie dell'Orologio 191 - Via Forte Marghera 101 - Mestre - ☎ 662411

Banco di Sicilia - S. Marco 5051 v. 2 Aprile - ☎ 707033

Banco San Marco - S. Marco 383 - ☎ 5289880

Cassa di Risparmio di Venezia - S. Marco 4216 Cp. Manin - ☎ 707644

Credito Italiano - Campo S. Salvador - ☎ 5289540

Istituto Bancario Italiano - S. Marco 1126 Bacino Orseolo - ☎ 962533

Istituto Federale Casse di Risparmio - Cf. S. Vidal 2847 - ☎ 705111

Istituto Mobiliare Italiano - Dorsoduro 1057 S. Trovaso - ☎ 5229403/5200117

Mediocredito delle Venezie - Cannaregio 3935 - ☎ 703388

HOTELS

VENICE

Area Code: 041
Zip Code: 30100

☆ ☆ ☆ ☆ ☆

Bauer Grunwald & Grand Hotel ☎ 707022 S. Marco Campo S. Moisè 1459

Cipriani ☎ 707744 Giudecca 10

Danieli ☎ 26480 Castello Riva degli Schiavoni 4196

Europa & Regina ☎ 700477 S. Marco Via XXII Marzo 2159

Gritti Palace ☎ 794611 S. Marco S. Maria del Giglio 2467

☆ ☆ ☆ ☆

Carlton Executive ☎ 718488 S. Croce S. Simeon Piccolo 578

Cavalletto & Doge Orseolo ☎ 700955 S. Marco Calle Cavalletto 1107

Etap Park Hotel ☎ 85394 S. Croce Fondamenta Condulmer 245

Gabrielli Sandwirth ☎ 5231580 Via Riva degli Schiavoni 4110

Londra Palace ☎ 700533 Castello Riva degli Schiavoni 4171

Luna ☎ 89840 S. Marco Calle dell'Ascensione 1243

Metropole ☎ 705044 Castello Riva degli Schiavoni 4149

Monaco & Grand Canal ☎ 700211 S. Marco Calle Vallaresso 1325

Principe ☎ 715022 Cannaregio Lista di Spagna 146

Saturnia & International ☎ 708377 Via XXII Marzo 2398

Splendid Suisse ☎ 700755 S. Marco Ponte dei Baretteri 760

☆ ☆ ☆

Ala ☎ 708333 S. Marco S. Maria del Giglio 2494

All'Angelo ☎ 709299 S. Marco Calle dell'Angelo 403

Al Sole Palace ☎ 32144 S. Croce Fondamenta Minotto 136

American ☎ 704733 Dorsoduro S. Vio 628

Austria & De La Ville ☎ 715300 Cannaregio Lista di Spagna 227

Bel Sito & Berlino ☎ 5223365 S. Marco S. Maria del Giglio 2517

Bisanzio ☎ 703100 Castello Calle della Pietà 3651

Bonvecchiati ☎ 85017 S. Marco Calle Goldoni 4488

Boston ☎ 87665 S. Marco Calle dei Fabbri 848

Capri ☎ 718988 S. Croce Corte del Gesù e Maria 595

Carpaccio ☎ 35946 S. Polo Calle Corner 2765

Casanova ☎ 706855 S. Marco Frezzeria 1284

Castello ☎ 5230217 Castello SS. Filippo e Giacomo 4365

Concordia ☎ 706866 S. Marco Calle Larga S. Marco 367

Continental ☎ 715122 Cannaregio Lista di Spagna 166

Corso ☎ 716422 Cannaregio Lista di Spagna 119

De L'Alboro ☎ 706977 S. Marco Corte dell'Alboro 3894/B

Do Pozzi ☎ 707855 S. Marco Corte do Pozzi 2373

Flora ☎ 705844 S. Marco Calle Bergamaschi 2283/A

Gardena ☎ 35549 S. Croce Fondamenta Tolentini 239

Giorgione ☎ 25810 Cannaregio SS. Apostoli 4587

Graspo de Ua ☎ 705644 S. Marco Calle dei Bombaseri 5094

Kette ☎ 707766 S. Marco 2053

La Fenice et des Artistes ☎ 32333 S. Marco Campiello Fenice 1936

Locanda Cipriani ☎ 730150 Isola di Torcello 29

Malibran ☎ 28028 Cannaregio S. Giov. Crisostomo 5864

Montecarlo ☎ 707144 S. Marco Calle Specchieri 463

Panada ☎ 709088 S. Marco Calle Specchieri 646

Patria & Tre Rose ☎ 5222490 S. Marco Calle dei Fabbri 905

Rialto ☎ 709166 S. Marco Riva del Ferro 5147

San Cassiano-Ca' Favretto ☎ 5223051 S. Croce Calle della Rosa 2232

San Marco ☎ 704277 P.za S. Marco 877

Santa Chiara ☎ 706955 S. Croce P.le Roma 548

Savoia & Jolanda ☎ 706644 Castello Riva degli Schiavoni 4187

Scandinavia ☎ 705965 Via S. Maria Formosa 5240

Terminus ☎ 715095 Cannaregio Lista di Spagna 116/A

Torino ☎ 705222 S. Marco Calle delle Ostreghe 2356

Union ☎ 715055 Cannaregio Lista di Spagna 127

Universo & Nord ☎ 715076 Cannaregio Lista di Spagna 121

☆ ☆

Abbazia ☎ 717333 Cannaregio Calle Priuli 66

Accademia-Villa Maravegie ☎ 5237846 Dorsoduro Fondamenta Bollani 1058

Adriatico ☎ 715176 Cannaregio Lista di Spagna 224

Agli Alboretti ☎ 5230058 Dorsoduro Rio Terrà S. Agnese 882/4

Airone ☎ 704800 S. Croce S. Simeon Piccolo 557

Alla Fava ☎ 29224 Castello Campo alla Fava 5525

All'Angelo ☎ 5222000 S. Marco Calle Larga S. Marco 381

Al Nuovo Teson ☎ 705555 Castello Campiello Pescaria 3980

Astoria ☎ 25381 S. Marco Calle Fiubera 951

Ateneo ☎ 700588 S. Marco S. Fantin 1876

Atlantico ☎ 709244 Castello Calle Rimedio 4416

Atlantide ☎ 716901 Cannaregio Calle Misericordia 375/A

Bartolomeo ☎ 35387 S. Marco-Rialto 5494

Basilea ☎ 718477 S. Croce Rio Marin 817

Brooklyn ☎ 5223227 S. Marco Calle dei Fabbri 4712

Ca' D'Oro ☎ 34797 Cannaregio Strada Nuova 4391/A

Campiello ☎ 35643 Castello S. Zaccaria 4647

Canada ☎ 29912 Castello Campo S. Lio 5659

Canal ☎ 5238480 S. Croce S. Simeon Piccolo 553

Caprera ☎ 715271 Cannaregio Lista di Spagna 219

Casa Fontana ☎ 710533 Castello Campo S. Provolo 4701

Casa Frollo ☎ 5222723 Giudecca Fondamenta Zitelle 50

Casa Igea ☎ 706644 Castello S. Zaccaria 4684

Centauro ☎ 25832 S. Marco Campo Manin 4297/a

Città di Milano ☎ 27002 S. Marco Campiello S. Zulian 590

Da Bruno ☎ 5230452 Castello Salizzada S. Lio 5726

Diana ☎ 709166 S. Marco Calle Specchieri 449

Dolomiti ☎ 715113 Cannaregio Calle Priuli 73

Falier ☎ 28882 S. Croce Salizzada S. Pantalon 130

Firenze ☎ 5222858 S. Marco Salizzada S. Moisè 1490

Florida ☎ 715253 Cannaregio Calle Priuli 106

Gallini ☎ 5236371 S. Marco Calle della Verona 3673

Gorizia-A la Valigia ☎ 5223737 S. Marco Calle dei Fabbri 4696/A

Guerrini ☎ 715333 Cannaregio Lista di Spagna 265

Iris ☎ 5222882 S. Polo S. Tomà 2910/A

La Calcina ☎ 706466 Dorsoduro Zattere 780

La Forcola ☎ 720277 B16 Cannaregio Rio Terrà Maddalena 2356

La Residenza ☎ 85315 Castello Campo Bandiera e Moro 3608

Leonardo ☎ 718666 Cannaregio Rio Terrà S. Leonardo 1385

Lisbona ☎ 86774 S. Marco Calle Barozzi 2153

Lux ☎ 35767 Castello Calle delle Rasse 4541

Madonna dell'Orto ☎ 719955 Cannaregio Fondamenta Madonna dell'Orto 3499

Marconi & Milano ☎ 5222068 S. Polo Riva del Vin 729

Mercurio ☎ 5220947 S. Marco Calle dei Barcaroli 1848

Mignon ☎ 5237388 Cannaregio SS. Apostoli 4535

Nazionale ☎ 716133 Cannaregio 158

Noemi ☎ 5238144 S. Marco Calle dei Fabbri 909

Olimpia ☎ 26141 S. Croce Fondamenta Burchielle 395

Paganelli ☎ 24324 Castello Riva degli Schiavoni 4182

Pausania ☎ 5222083 Dorsoduro S. Barnaba 2824

Pellegrino & Commercio ☎ 707922 Castello Calle delle Rasse 4551

Piazzale Roma ☎ 703065 S. Croce Treponti 390

San Fantin ☎ 5231401 S. Marco Campiello Fenice 1930/A

San Gallo ☎ 27311 S. Marco Campo S. Gallo 1093/A

San Maurizio ☎ 89712 S. Marco S. Maurizio 2624

San Moisé ☎ 703755 S. Marco 2058

San Stefano ☎ 700166 S. Marco Campo S. Stefano 2957

Seguso ☎ 5222340 Dorsoduro Zattere 779

Serenissima ☎ 700011 S. Marco Calle Goldoni 4486

Spagna ☎ 715011 Cannaregio Lista di Spagna 184

Stella Alpina/Edelweiss ☎ 715179 Cannaregio Calle Priuli 99/D

Tivoli ☎ 5222656 Dorsoduro Crosera S. Pantalon 3838

Trovatore ☎ 5224611 Castello Calle delle Rasse 4534

Walter ☎ 86204 S. Croce Fondamenta Tolentini 240

Zecchini ☎ 715611 Cannaregio Lista di Spagna 152

Adua ☎ 716184 Cannaregio Lista di Spagna 233/A

Ai due Fanali ☎ 718344 S. Croce S. Simeon Grande 946

Alex ☎ 5231341 S. Paolo Rio Terrà Frari 2606

Al Gambero ☎ 5224384 S. Marco Calle 4687

Al Gazzettino ☎ 86523 S. Marco Calle delle Acque 4971

Al Gobbo ☎ 715001 Cannaregio Campo S. Geremia 312

Alla Salute-Da Cici ☎ 35404 Dorsoduro Fondamenta Ca' Balà 222

Alle Guglie ☎ 717351 Cannaregio S. Leonardo 1523

Al Piave-Da Mario ☎ 85174 Castello Ruga Giuffa 4840

Antiche Figure ☎ 718290 S. Croce S. Simeon Piccolo 686

Antico Capon ☎ 85292 Dorsoduro Campo S. Margherita 3004

Basilea ☎ 718667 S. Croce Rio Marin 804

Belvedere ☎ 85148 Castello Via Garibaldi 1636

Bernardi Semenzato ☎ 27257 Cannaregio SS. Apostoli 4366

Bridge ☎ 705287 Castello SS. Filippo e Giacomo 4498

Bucintoro ☎ 5223240 Castello Riva S. Biagio 2135/A

Budapest ☎ 5220514 S. Marco Corte Barozzi 2143

Ca' Foscari ☎ 25817 Dorsoduro Calle della Frescada 3888

Canal ☎ 5238480 Castello Fond.ta Remedio 4422/C

Canaletto ☎ 5220518 Castello S. Lio 5487

Caneva ☎ 28118 Castello Ramo della Fava 5515

Casa Boccassini ☎ 29892 Cannaregio Calle del Fumo 5295

Casa Carettoni ☎ 716231 Cannaregio Lista di Spagna 130

Casa de Stefani ☎ 5223337 Dorsoduro Calle Traghetto S. Barnaba 2786

Casa Messner ☎ 27443 Dorsoduro Salute 216/237

Casa Peron ☎ 86038 S. Croce Calle dei Vinanti 85

Casa Petrarca ☎ 700430 S. Marco Calle delle Colonne 4394

Casa Verardo ☎ 86127 Castello Ruga Giuffa 4765

Città di Berna ☎ 25872 S. Marco S. Zulian 535

Corona ☎ 29174 Castello Calle Corona 4464

Da Bepi ☎ 26735 S. Croce Fondamenta Minotto 160

Dalla Mora ☎ 35703 S. Croce Salizzada S. Pantalon 42/A-44

Da Pino ☎ 5223646 Dorsoduro Crosera S. Pantalon 3942

Doni ☎ 5224267 Castello S. Zaccaria 4656

Eden ☎ 720228 Cannaregio Rio Terrà Maddalena 2357

Fiorita ☎ 34754 S. Marco Campiello Nuovo 3457/A

Guerrato ☎ 27131 S. Polo Calle dietro la Scimmia 240/A

Hesperia ☎ 715251 Cannaregio Fondamenta S. Giobbe 459

Marin ☎ 718022 S. Croce Calle del Traghetto 670/B

Marte ☎ 716351 Cannaregio Ponte delle Guglie 338

Massimo-Felix ☎ 5236722 S. Marco Calle dei Fabbri 981

Minerva e Nettuno ☎ 715968 Cannaregio Lista di Spagna 230

Moderno ☎ 716679 Cannaregio Lista di Spagna 154/B

Montin ☎ 27151 Dorsoduro Fond.ta di Borgo 1147

Orion ☎ 5223053 S. Marco Spadaria 700/A

Raspo de Ua ☎ 730095 Isola di Burano Via Galuppi 560

Rio ☎ 34810 Castello SS. Filippo e Giacomo 4356

Riva ☎ 27034 Castello Ramo Casselleria 5310

Rossi ☎ 715164 Cannaregio Calle delle Procuratie 262

San Geremia ☎ 716245 Cannaregio Campo S. Geremia 290

San Giorgio ☎ 35835 S. Marco Calle della Mandola 3781

San Salvador ☎ 89147 S. Marco Calle Galiazza 5264

San Samuele ☎ 28045 S. Marco Piscina S. Samuele 3358

Santa Lucia ☎ 715180 Cannaregio Calle Misericordia 358

Sant'Anna ☎ 704203 Castello S. Anna 269

Silva ☎ 27643 Castello Fondamenta Remedio 4423

Stefania ☎ 703757 S. Croce Tolentini 181/A

Sturion ☎ 5236243 S. Paolo Calle del Sturion 679

Tiepolo ☎ 5231315 Castello SS. Filippo e Giacomo 4510

Tintoretto ☎ 700874 Cannaregio S. Fosca 2316

Toscana Tofanelli ☎ 35722 Castello Via Garibaldi 1650

Vagon ☎ 85626 Cannaregio Campiello Selvatico 5619

Villa Rosa ☎ 716569 Cannaregio Calle Misericordia 389

Wildner ☎ 27463 Castello Riva degli Schiavoni 4161

VENICE - LIDO OF VENICE

☆ ☆ ☆ ☆ ☆

Excelsior ☎ 5260201 Lungomare Marconi 41

☆ ☆ ☆ ☆

Des Bains ☎ 765921 Lungomare Marconi 17

Quattro Fontane ☎ 768814 Via 4 Fontane 16

Villa Mabapa ☎ 5260590 Riviera S. Niccolò 16

☆ ☆ ☆

Biasutti Adria Urania-Nora ☎ 5260120 Via E. Dandolo 29
Biasutti Villa Ada ☎ 5261447 Via E. Dandolo 24
Buon Pesce ☎ 5260533 Riviera S. Nicolò 49
Cappelli's ☎ 5260140 Via Perasto 5
Centrale & Byron ☎ 5260052 Via M. Bragadin 30
Helvetia ☎ 5260105 Gran Viale 4/6
Hungaria ☎ 5261212 Gran Viale 28
La Meridiana ☎ 5260343 Via Lepanto 45
Petit Palais ☎ 765993 Lungomare Marconi 54
Rigel ☎ 768810 Via E. Dandolo 13
Riviera ☎ 5260031 Gran Viale 5
Villa Otello ☎ 5260048 Via Lepanto 12

☆ ☆

Atlanta-Augustus ☎ 5260569 Via Lepanto 15
Belvedere ☎ 5260115 Via Cerigo 1
Cristallo ☎ 765293 Gran Viale 51

Panorama ☎ 5260378 S.M. Elisabetta 1
Reiter ☎ 5260107 Gran Viale 57
Rivamare ☎ 5260352 Lungomare Marconi 44
Sorriso ☎ 5260729 Via Colombo 22/C
Vianello ☎ 731072 Alberoni Via Ca' Rossa 10
Villa Albertina ☎ 5260879 Via Vallaresso 1
Villa Aurora ☎ 5260519 Riviera S. Nicolò 11/A
Villa Cipro ☎ 5261408 Via Zara 2
Villa Laguna ☎ 5260342 Via S. Gallo 6
Villa Pannonia ☎ 5260162 Via D. Michiel 1

☆

Edera ☎ 5260791 Via Negroponte 13
Giardinetto ☎ 5260801 S.M. Elisabetta 3
La Pergola ☎ 5260784 Via Cipro 15
Stella ☎ 5260745 Via S. Gallo 111
Villa delle Palme ☎ 5261312 Via E. Dandolo 12
Villa Mirella ☎ 5260393 Via Dardanelli 29
Villa Parco ☎ 5260015 Via Rodi 1
Villa Tiziana ☎ 5261193 Via Gritti 3

VENICE - CAVALLINO

☆ ☆ ☆ ☆ ☆

Fenix ☎ 968040 Via F. Baracca 45
Lio Grando ☎ 966136 Punta Sabbioni P.le Lio Grando
Union Lido ☎ 968043 Via Fausta 270

☆ ☆

Ca' di Valle Junior ☎ 968123 Ca' di Valle C.so Italia 10
International ☎ 968108 Ca' di Valle C.so Italia 15
La Rondine ☎ 966172 Punta Sabbioni Via Fausta 60
Righetto ☎ 968083 Ca' di Valle C.so Italia 16
Sole Mare ☎ 968023 Via Fausta 345
Valdor ☎ 966108 Ca' Savio Via Meduna 5

☆

Al Buon Pesce-Da Aldo ☎ 968064 Via Fausta 605/A
Al Capitello ☎ 968012 Via Fausta 412
Al Cason ☎ 968036 Ca' di Valle Corso Europa
Al Gondoliere-Bavaria ☎ 966008 Ca' Savio Via Fausta 152
Al Ponte ☎ 968025 Via Fausta 484
Ca' di Valle ☎ 968123 Ca' di Valle Via Fausta 298
Cavallino Bianco ☎ 968018 Ca' di Valle Via Fausta 304
Da Achille ☎ 968005 P.za S. Maria Elisabetta 16
Da Giovanni ☎ 968063 Via del Faro 603
Da Scarpa ☎ 966428 Punta Sabbioni Via Pealto 17
Laura ☎ 968029 Ca' Ballarin Via Costanziaca 3
Primavera ☎ 966005 Treporti Via Fausta 98
Rosa ☎ 968086 Via F. Baracca 36
Safari ☎ 966101 Ca' Pasquali Via Batterie 160
Villa Gentile ☎ 966019 Ca' Savio Via Mare 25
Zanella ☎ 966011 Treporti P.za Trinità 6

VENICE - MARGHERA

☆ ☆ ☆ ☆

Motelagip ☎ 936900 Via della Fonte 20

☆ ☆ ☆

Lugano Torretta ☎ 936777 Via Rizzardi 11
Mondial ☎ 930099 Via Rizzardi 21

Vienna ☎ 936600 Via Rizzardi 54

☆ ☆

Bianca ☎ 923656 Via G.le Cantore 23
Colombo ☎ 920711 Via Paolucci
Lloyd ☎ 930798 Via Rizzardi 32
Piccolo ☎ 920632 Via Trieste 2/H
Touring ☎ 920122 Via Paolucci 4
Villa Graziella ☎ 921655 Via Coletti 6

☆

Adele ☎ 920376 P.za S. Antonio 5
Amba Alagi ☎ 921728 Via Mutilati del Lavoro 38
Autostrada ☎ 921403 Via Trieste 1
Bandiera ☎ 927477 Via F.lli Bandiera 90
Belvedere ☎ 926596 Via Mezzacapo 1

Colombo Dip. ☎ 920711 Via Grondoni 1
Martello ☎ 926569 P.le Mezzacapo 3
Rana ☎ 920459 Via F.lli Bandiera 192
Risorta ☎ 923740 Via Colombara 2
Rizzardi ☎ 923416 Via Rizzardi 67
Roma ☎ 921967 Via Beccaria 1
Romano ☎ 935498 Via Minotto 2

VENICE - MESTRE

☆ ☆ ☆ ☆

Ambasciatori ☎ 5310699 C.so del Popolo 221
Michelangelo ☎ 986600 Via Forte Marghera 69

☆ ☆ ☆

Albatros ☎ 611000 V.le Don Sturzo 32
Bologna & Stazione ☎ 931000 Via Piave 214
Capitol ☎ 984783 Via Orlanda 1
Plaza ☎ 929388 P.le Stazione 36
President ☎ 985655 Via Forte Marghera 99/A
Sirio ☎ 949194 Via Circonvallazione 109
Tritone ☎ 930955 Via Stazione 15

☆ ☆

Alla Giustizia ☎ 913955 Via Miranese 111
Aquila Nera ☎ 611088 Favaro Veneto Via Essiccatoio 38
Ariston ☎ 972293 Via Terraglio 11/C
Aurora ☎ 989832 P.tta G. Bruno 15
Centrale ☎ 985522 P.le Donatori di Sangue 15
Da Mario ☎ 964022 Tessera Via Triestina 170
Delle Rose ☎ 951711 Via Millosevich 46
Ducale ☎ 630400 Favaro Veneto Via Triestina 5
Garibaldi ☎ 968162 V.le Garibaldi 24
Kappa ☎ 957133 Carpenedo Via Trezzo 6
Marco Polo ☎ 900344 Campalto Via Orlanda 332
Nuova Mestre ☎ 913803 Chirignago Via Liguria 4
Piave ☎ 929477 Via Col Moschin 10
San Carlo ☎ 970912 Via Forte Marghera 131
San Giuliano ☎ 957604 Via Forte Marghera 193/A
Venezia ☎ 985533 Via Teatro Vecchio 5

Vittoria ☎ 616655 Carpenedo Via S. Donà 76
Vivit ☎ 951385 P.za Ferretto 75

☆

Adria ☎ 989755 Via Cappuccina 34
Alla Torre ☎ 984646 Calle del Sale 54
Alle Colonnette ☎ 631555 Favaro Veneto Via Altinia 72
Al Veronese ☎ 926275 Via Cappuccina 94/A
Aquila Nera Dip. ☎ 611124 Favaro Veneto Via Staulanza 2
Cavallino ☎ 940314 Via S. Donà 39
Col di Lana ☎ 926879 Via Fagarè 19
Corso ☎ 930075 C.so del Popolo 231
Cortina ☎ 929206 Via Piave 153
Cris ☎ 926773 Via Monte Nero 3
Da Giacomo ☎ 610536 Favaro Veneto Via Altinia 49
Da Mario Dip. ☎ 964022 Tessera Via Triestina 170
Da Tito ☎ 932390 Via Cappuccina 69
Dina ☎ 926565 Via Parini 4
Giovannina ☎ 926396 Via Dante 113
Johnny ☎ 964093 Tessera Via Orlanda 223
La Boheme ☎ 964170 Tessera Via Orlanda 258
La Triestina ☎ 900168 Campalto Via Orlanda 62
Lucy ☎ 900748 Campalto Via Cimitero 14
Maria Luisa ☎ 931968 Via Parini 2
Mary ☎ 900219 Campalto Via Orlanda 152
Montepiana ☎ 926242 Via Monte S. Michele 17
Montiron ☎ 964068 Favaro Veneto Via Triestina 246
Paris ☎ 926037 V.le Venezia 11
Primavera ☎ 974511 Via Orlanda 5
Riva ☎ 972566 Via Pescheria 24/B
Roberta ☎ 929355 Via Sernaglia 21
Trento ☎ 926090 Via Fagarè 2
Trieste ☎ 929462 Via Trento 8/2

Distributor for Venice:
BENEDETTI SOUVENIRS S.a.s. di Benedetti Stefano & C.
Via Cannaregio 3548/49
30121 VENICE
Tel. (041) 71.87.82 - 72.09.77   Fax (041) 52.40.767

© Copyright 1995 by Bonechi Edizioni "Il Turismo" S.r.l.
Via dei Rustici, 5
50122 FLORENCE
Tel. (055) 239.82.24 - Fax (055) 21.63.66
Photos: Paolo Bacherini (page 7, 16, 17, 19, 20, 21, 22, 23, 25, 27, 28, 30, 32, 40, 41, 43, 47, 49, 50, 60, 62, 64, 65, 98, 106)
Printed in Italy
All rights reserved
ISBN 88-7204-167-8